E. S. Brooks

Historic Boys

Brooks, E. S.

Historic Boys

ISBN/EAN: 978-3-86741-458-6
First published in 2010 by Europaeischer Hochschulverlag GmbH &
Co KG, Bremen, Germany.

© Europaeischer Hochschulverlag GmbH & Co KG, Fahrenheitstr.
1, D-28359 Bremen (www.ehv-online.com). All rights reserved.

This book is a reproduction of an out of print title and has originally
been published in 1886. Because no electronic master copies of this
title could be obtained, the publisher had to reuse old copies of the
text. We therefore apologize for any possible loss in quality.

E. S. Brooks

Historic Boys

Preface.

The world's historic boys and girls have been many. In every age and clime may be found notable examples of young people who, even before they reached manhood or womanhood, have — for good or evil — left their impress on their time.

From these the author of this volume has selected the careers of a dozen young fellows of different lands and epochs, who, even had they not lived out their "teens," could have rightly claimed a place in the world's annals as Historic Boys. They are such also as show that, from the earliest ages, manliness and self-reliance have ever been the chief groundwork of character, and that in this respect the boy of the nineteenth century in no way differs from his brother of the second or the ninth. To bravely front danger, difficulty, or death, if need be, for principle or right, is as commendable and as heroic in the boy brought up amid the surging and restless life of London to-day, as in the lads who trod the narrow streets of Jerusalem, or Rouen, of Florence, or old Rome centuries ago.

These stories of boy life, in the stirring days of old, have been based upon historic facts and prepared with a due regard to historic and chronologic accuracy. Nine of the twelve stories have already appeared in *St. Nicholas* magazine, but these have been revised and amplified for their present use, while the remaining three were specially prepared for this volume.

CONTENTS.

I. Marcus Of Rome: The Boy Magistrate. 2
II. Brian Of Munster: The Boy Chieftain. 20
III. Olaf Of Norway: The Boy Viking. 35
IV. William Of Normandy: The Boy Knight. 51
V. Baldwin Of Jerusalem: The Boy Crusader. 66
VI. Frederick Of Hohenstaufen: The Boy Emperor. 82
VII. Harry Of Monmouth: The Boy General. 99
VIII. Giovanni Of Florence, The Boy Cardinal. 121
IX. Ixtlil' Of Tezcuco — The Boy Cacique. 138
X. Louis Of Bourbon, The Boy King. 153
XI. Charles Of Sweden: The Boy Conqueror. 169
XII. Van Rensselaer Of Rensselaerswyck: The Boy Patroon. 187

LIST OF ILLUSTRATIONS.

Marcus Annius Verus, Afterward The Emperor Marcus Aurelius Antoninus.	1
Lictors.	6
Annia, The Sister Of Marcus, And Her Pets.	13
"The Boy Chieftain Knelt And Kissed The Hem Of The Darling Little Maiden's Purple Robe."	29
The Castle Of Falaise — Birthplace Of William The Conqueror.	55
"So, Hollo, My Lord Duke," Said Hubert, "What Taketh Thee Abroad In This Guise So Early?"	60
"Thou The King!" He Exclaimed; "Thou That Baldwin Of Jerusalem Whom Men Do Call The Hero Of The Jordan!"	70
Conrad the Emperor quitting the Crusade.	79
"Cross At Thy Peril, Baron Kapparon," Cried Frederick Of Hohenstaufen.	85
Prince Henry Picks Up The Gage Of The Percies' Defiance. — "This Shall Be My Duty," He Said.	110
Haulpilli The Lord Of Tezcuco Reveals Himself, — "Now Who Shall Say Me Nay?" He Asked.	142
"I'll Make Them Rue Their Words Ere This Day's Sun Cross The Dome Of The Smoking Hill."	147
Eagle-Flag Of Sweden.	183
"Suppawn And Malck And Rulliches, With Chocolate And Soft Waffles, You Know," Said Mistress Margery.	195
"The Throng Of Tenants Greeted Him With A Rousing Birthday Cheer."	198

Marcus Annius Verus, Afterward The Emperor Marcus Aurelius Antoninus.

I. MARCUS OF ROME: THE BOY MAGISTRATE.

(Afterward the Emperor Marcus Aurelius Antoninus.)
A.D. 137.

A perfect autumn day. Above, the clear sky of Italy; below, a grassy plain, sloping gently down from the brown cliffs and ruined ramparts of old Veii — the city of the ancient Tuscan kings. In the background, under the shade of the oaks, a dozen waiting attendants; and here, in the open space before us, three trim and sturdy Roman youths, all flushed with the exercise of a royal game of ball. Come, boys and girls of to-day, go back with me seventeen and a half centuries, and join the dozen lookers-on as they follow this three-cornered game of ball. They call it the *trigon*. It is a favorite ball-game with the Roman youth, in which the three players, standing as if on a right-angled triangle, pitch and catch the ball, or *pila*, at long distances and with the left hand only. It is not so easy as you may think. Try it some time and see for yourself.

"This way — toss it this way, Aufidius; our good Sejus will need more lessons from old Trimalchio, the gladiator, ere he outranks us at *trigon*."

And with a quick but guarded dash of the left hand the speaker caught the ball as it came spinning toward him, and with as vigorous a "left-hander" sent it flying across to young Sejus.

"Faith, my Marcus," said Sejus, as he caught the ball with difficulty, "the gallop from Lorium has made me somewhat stiff of joint, and I pitch and catch but poorly. Keep the *pila* flying, and I may grow more elastic, though just now I feel much like our last text from Epictetus, that the good Rusticus gave us yesterday — 'a little soul bearing about a corpse.'"

"What then! Art as stiff as that, old Sejus?" gayly shouted Aufidius. "Ho! brace thee up, man," he cried, as he sent the ball whirling across to Marcus; "brace thee up, and use rather the words of our wise young Stoic here — 'Be like the promontory against which the waves continually break, but it stands firm and tames the fury of the waters around it.'"

"'T is well applied, Aufidius. But — said I all that?" Marcus inquired.

"Ay, so didst thou, my Marcus. 'T is all down on my tablets." And with merry talk the game went on.

But soon old Ballio, the *ordinarius*, or upper servant, left the oak shade and said to Marcus: "Come, my master; the water-glass shows that we must soon ride on if we mean to reach Rome by dinner-time."

So the game was broken off, and, after a few nibbles at the cakes and sweetmeats which one of the slaves carried to "stay the stomachs" of the travellers, the call "To horse!" was given, and the party moved on toward the city. The spirits of the lads ran high; and though the one called Marcus had a sedate and quiet look, he was roused into healthy and hearty boyishness as, over the Etruscan plains, they galloped on to Rome.

They had been riding, perhaps, a short half hour, when they saw, coming down a cross-road that entered the highway just beyond them, a large flock of sheep returning from their summer pasturage on the hills, in charge of three shepherds and their families. The game and the gallop had made the boys ripe for mischief; for, though close and patient students, they were in their hours of sport as ready for a frolic as are any schoolboys of to-day.

The shepherds, seeing a party of hard riders coming toward them, looked at their sheep anxiously and eyed the strangers suspiciously. For sheep-stealing was of common occurrence in those days, and, when changing pastures, the shepherds were kept constantly on the watch.

The quick eye of Aufidius marked the suspicions of the shepherds.

"Why, Marcus," he exclaimed, "yonder fellows surely take us for highwaymen."

"Highwaymen, indeed!" said Sejus, indignantly. "Dost think the knaves could mistake the noble Marcus Verus for a cowardly sheep-stealer."

"And why not," said Marcus, laughingly. "Man looks at man but as his reason bids him. If shepherds look but for sheep-stealers, to them, at first, all men are sheep-stealers. Come," he added, gayly, "let us not disappoint them. What did our teacher Rusticus tell us but yesterday: 'That which is a hinderance is made a furtherance to an act, and that which is an obstacle on the road helps us on the road.' Shall we not put his text to the test? Behold our obstacle on the road! Let us ride down the sheep!"

The spirit of mischief is contagious. Down the highway dashed the whole party, following the lead of Marcus and his cry of "Forward, friends!" while the now terrified shepherds turned their huddling sheep around, and with many cries and much belaboring struggled back to the cross-road to escape the pretended robbers. But the swift horses soon overtook the slow-footed shepherds, and the laughing riders, with uplifted weapons and shouts of seeming victory, were quickly at the heels of the flock. Then came a change. The shepherds, finding that they could not outrun their pursuers, stopped, wheeled around, and stood on the defensive, laying valiantly about them with crook and staff.

"'Go on and increase in valor, O boy! this is the path to immortality,'" shouted the nimble Aufidius, and with this quotation from Virgil, he swooped down and caught up a struggling lamb.

"What says your philosophy now, O Marcus?" said Sejus as, rather ruefully, he rubbed an aching shin, sore from the ringing thwack of a shepherd's crook.

Marcus dodged a similar blow and replied "That nothing happens to any man, O Sejus, which he is not fitted by nature to bear. But I have had enough. Let us go our way in peace."

And turning from the fray, the whole party rode rather ingloriously from the field of defeat, while the victors vowed a lamb to Pales, the special patroness of shepherds, for their deliverance from "so blood-thirsty" a band of robbers.

So, flushed and merry over their adventure, the three lads

rode on to Rome; but, ere they came in sight of the yellow Tiber, a fleet Numidian slave came running toward them, straight and swift as an arrow, right in the middle of the highway. Marcus recognized him as one of the runners of his uncle, the proconsul Titus Antoninus, and wondered as to his mission. The Numidian stopped short at sight of the party, and, saluting Marcus, handed him a small scroll. The boy unrolled it, and at once his face became grave.

"For me; this for me?" he said, and, in seeming surprise, laid his hand upon the arm of his friend Aufidius. Then, as if remembering that he was a Stoic, whose desire was to show neither surprise, pleasure, nor pain, let what might happen, he read the scroll carefully, placed it in his mantle, and said, half aloud: "How ridiculous is he who is surprised at any thing which happens in life!"

"What is it that so disturbs you, O Marcus?" Aufidius asked.

"Friends," said the lad, "this scroll from my uncle Antoninus tells me that I am named by the Emperor's council as prefect [1] of the city while the consuls and magistrates are at the Latin Games."

"Hail to thee, Prefect! hail! hail! hail!" cried Aufidius and Sejus, while the whole company joined in a respectful salute.

"Would it were some one more worthy than I, Aufidius," said Marcus, solemnly.

"Nay, it is rightly decreed, my Marcus," protested his friend, proudly. "Did not Hadrian, the Emperor, himself say of thee: '*Non Verus, sed Verissimus!*' [2] and who but thee, Marcus Verissimus — Marcus the most true — should be the governor of Rome?"

"But think of it, friends! I am but a boy after all. Who can respect a prefect of sixteen?" still queried the modest Marcus.

Sejus at once dipped into history.

"And why not, O Marcus?" he asked. "Was not Tiberius Cæsar a public orator at nine, and Augustus a master of the horse at seventeen? Was not Titus a quæstor [3] before he was eighteen, and the great Julius himself a priest of Jupiter at fourteen? And why, then, should not Marcus Verus, in whose veins runs the blood of the ancient kings, rightly be prefect of the city at sixteen?"

"Thou art a good pleader, my Sejus," Marcus said pleasantly. "Since, then, I must be prefect, may I be a just one, and take for my motto the text of the good Rusticus: 'If it is not right, do not do it; if it is not true, do not say it.' So, forward, my good friends! The lictors await me at the city gate."

Lictors.

So they pressed forward and, with more decorum, rode along the Via Cassia and across the Milvian Bridge to the broader Via Lata and the city gate. Here an escort of six lictors with their rods of office welcomed Marcus, and, thus accompanied, the young magistrate passed down the Via Lata — the street now known as "the Corso," the great thoroughfare of modern Rome —

to the palace of his uncle Antoninus, near the Cœlian Gate.

"Hail, Prefect!" came the welcome of the noble uncle (one of the grand characters of Roman history). "And how fare the hens of Lorium?" For the good proconsul, so soon to be hailed as Cæsar and Emperor, loved the country pleasures and country cares of his farm at Lorium more than all the sculptured magnificence of the imperial city.

"The hens are well conditioned, O Antoninus," answered the boy, simply.

"But what said I?" his uncle exclaimed gayly. "What cares a prefect of Rome for the scratching hens of Lorium? As for me, most noble Prefect, I am but a man from whom neither power nor philosophy can take my natural affections"; and, as the parrot swinging over the door-way croaked out his "*Salve!*" (Welcome!), arm-in-arm uncle and nephew entered the palace.

Marcus Annius Verus was in all respects a model boy. Not the namby-pamby model that all human boys detest, but a right-minded, right-mannered, healthy, wealthy, and wise young Roman of the second century of the Christian era. At that time (for the world was not yet Christianized) there flourished a race of teachers and philosophers known as Stoics — wise old pagans, who held that the perfect man must be free from passion, unmoved by either joy or grief, taking every thing just as it came, with supreme and utter indifference. A hard rule that, but this lad's teachers had been mainly of the "School of the Stoics," as it was called, and their wise sayings had made so deep an impression on the little Marcus that, when only twelve years old, he set up for a full-fledged Stoic. He put on the coarse mantle that was the peculiar dress of the sect, practised all their severe rules of self-denial, and even slept on the hard floor or the bare ground, denying himself the comfort of a bed, until his good mother, who knew what was best for little fellows, even though they were Stoics, persuaded him to compromise on a quilt. He loved exercise and manly sport; but he was above all a wonderful student — too much of a student, in fact; for, as the old record states, "his excess in study was the only fault of his youth." And yet he loved a frolic, as the adventure with the shepherds proves.

Of the best patrician blood of old Rome; the relative and favorite of the great Emperor Hadrian; a splendid scholar, a capital gymnast, a true friend, a modest and unassuming lad; he was trying, even at sixteen, to make the best of himself, squaring all his actions by the rule that he, in after years, put into words: "I do my duty; other things trouble me not." Is not this young pagan of seventeen centuries back worthy to be held up as a model boy? Manly boys, with good principles, good manners, and good actions, are young gentlemen always, whenever and wherever they may live; and quickly enough, as did young Marcus of Rome, they find their right place in the regard and affections of the people about them.

Well, the days of waiting have passed. The great festival to Jove, the *Feriæ Latinæ*, has drawn all the high magistrates to Mount Albanus, and in their stead, as prefect of the city, rules the boy Marcus. In one of the *basilicæ*, or law courts of the great Forum, he sits invested with the toga of office, the ring and the purple badge; and, while twelve sturdy lictors guard his curule chair, he listens to the cases presented to him and makes many wise decisions — "in which honor," says the old record, "he acquitted himself to the general approbation." It was here no doubt that he learned the wisdom of the words he wrote in after life: "Do not have such an opinion of things as he who does the wrong, or such as he wishes thee to have, but look at them as they are in truth."

"Most noble Prefect," said one of the court messengers, or *accensi*, as they were called, "there waits, without, one Lydus the herdsman, demanding justice."

"Bid him enter," said Marcus; and there came into the *basilica* one whose unexpected appearance brought consternation to Aufidius and Sejus, as they waited in the court, and caused even the calm face of Marcus to flush with surprise. Lydus the herdsman was none other than their old acquaintance, the shepherd of the Etruscan highway!

"Most noble Prefect," said the shepherd, with a low salutation, "I am a free herdsman of Lake Sabatinus, and I ask for justice against a band of terrible highwaymen who lurk on the Via Cassia, near to old Veii. Only three days since, did these lawless fellows beset me and my companions, with our flocks, on the highway, and cruelly rob and maltreat us. I pray thee, let the *cohortes vigilum* [4] search out and punish these robbers; and let me, too, be fully satisfied for the sheep they did force from me."

"Not so fast, man," said Marcus, as the shepherd concluded his glib recital. "Couldst thou identify these knaves, if once they were apprehended?"

"Ay, that could I, noble Prefect," replied the shepherd, boldly. "They were led on by three as villainous rascals as go unhung, and these had with them a crowd of riotous followers."

"Ha! is it so?" said Marcus. "Aufidius! Sejus! I pray you, step this way." His two friends, in some wonder as to his intention, approached the tribunal; and Marcus, stepping down from his curule chair, placed himself between them. "Three villainous rascals, thou didst say. Were they aught like us, think'st thou?"

"Like you? O noble young Prefect!" began the shepherd, protestingly. But when, at a word from Marcus, the three lads drew back their arms as if to brandish their weapons, and shouted their cry of attack, the mouth of Lydus stood wide open in amazement, his cropped head fairly bristled with fright, and, with a hasty exclamation, he turned on his heel, and fled from the *basilica*.

"Ho there, bring him back!" Marcus commanded; and guarded by two lictors, Lydus was dragged reluctantly back into the presence of the young prefect.

"So, my shepherd," said Marcus, "thou hast recognized thy villainous rascals. Surely, though, thy fear was larger than thine eyeballs; for thou didst multiply both the followers and the harm done to thee. Thou hast asked for justice, and justice thou shalt have! Forasmuch as I and my companions did frighten thee, though but in sport, it is wise to do well what doth seem but just. I, then, as prefect of the city, do fine Marcus Annius Verus, Aufidius Victorianus, and Sejus Fruscianus, each, one hundred *sestertii* (about twenty shillings), for interfering with travellers on the public highway; and I do command the lictors to mark the offenders unless they do straightway pay the fine here laid upon them."

Aufidius and Sejus looked troubled. They had barely a hundred *sestertii* between them; but Marcus drew forth an amount equal to the three fines, and, handing the money to an *accensus*, bade him pay the shepherd. With many a bow, Lydus accepted the money, and with the words, "O noble young Prefect! O wise beyond thy years!" he would have withdrawn again.

"Hold!" said Marcus, ascending the tribunal, "hear the rest! Because thou hast placed a false charge before this tribunal, and hast sought to profit by thy lying tongue, I, the Prefect, do command that thou dost pay over to the *scriba* (clerk of the court) the sum of three hundred *sestertii*, to be devoted to the service of the poor; and that thou dost wear the wooden collar until thy fine is paid."

Very soberly and ruefully, Lydus paid over as the price of his big stories exactly the sum which he had received from the *scriba*, and departed from the *basilica* of the boy prefect, if not a poorer, at least a sadder and a wiser man.

The days of Marcus' magistracy were soon over, and when the great festival of Jove was ended, and the magistrates had returned to the city, the lad gave up the curule chair and the dress and duties of his office, and retired to his mother's house, bearing with him the thanks of the magistrates, the approval of the Emperor, and the applause of the people.

The villa of the matron Domitia Lucilla, the mother of Marcus, stood embowered in delightful gardens on the Cœlian Hill, the most easterly of the famous Seven Hills of Rome. In an age of splendor, when grand palaces lined the streets and covered the hill-slopes of the imperial city, when fortunes were spent upon baths and gardens, or wasted on a gala dress, or on a single meal, this pleasant house was conducted upon a plan that suited the home ways of the mother and the quiet tastes of the son. Let us enter the spacious vestibule. Here in the door-way, or *ostium*, we stop to note the "*Salve!*" (Welcome!) wrought in mosaic on the marble floor, and then pass into the *atrium*, or great living-room of the house, where the female slaves are spinning deftly, and every thing tells of order and a busy life. Now, let us pass on to the spacious court-yard, in the very heart of the house. In the unroofed centre a beautiful fountain shoots its jets of cooling spray from a marble cistern of clear water.

And here, by the shining fountain, in the central court, stand two persons — Marcus and his mother. The lad has laid aside his *toga*, or outside mantle, and his close-fitting, short-sleeved tunic, scarcely reaching to his knees, shows a well-knit frame and a healthy, sun-browned skin. His mother, dressed in the tunic and long white *stola*, or outer robe, is of matronly presence and pleasant face. And, as they talk together in low and earnest tones, they watch with loving eyes, from the cool shadows of the high area walls, the motions of the dark-eyed little Annia, a winsome Roman maiden of thirteen, as, perched upon a cage of pet pigeons, she gleefully teases with a swaying peacock plume now the fluttering pigeons and now the wary-eyed Dido, her favorite cat.

"But there is such a thing as too much self-denial, my Marcus," said the mother in answer to some remark of the lad.

"Nay, this is not self-denial, my mother; it is simple justice," replied the boy. "Are not Annia and I children of the same father and mother? Is it just that I should receive all the benefit of our family wealth, and that she should be dependent on my bounty?"

"Divide then thy father's estate, my son. Let Annia and thyself share alike, but give it not all to thy sister," his mother suggested.

"'Receive wealth without arrogance and be ready to let it go,' is what the Stoic Commodus hath taught me," the boy replied. "To whom we love much we should be ready to give much. Is it not so, my mother?"

"So I believe, my son," the matron answered.

"And if I seek to act justly in this matter, shall I not follow thy counsels, my mother?" Marcus continued; "for thou hast said, 'No longer talk about the kind of a man a good man ought to be, but be such.'"

"Ah, Marcus," the pleased mother exclaimed, "thou wilt be a happy man, too, if thou canst go ever by the right way, and think and act in the right way, as now. Thou art a good youth."

"And what is goodness, mother," argued the young philosopher, "but the desire to do justice and to practise it, and in this to let desire end? Let me, then, as I desire, give all my father's estate to my sister Annia. My grandfather's is sufficient for my needs. So shall Annia have her fair marriage portion, and we, my mother, shall all be satisfied."

And now, his sister Annia, wearying of her play with the pigeons, dropped her peacock plume and ran merrily toward her brother.

"O Marcus," she cried, "'t will soon be time for the bath. Do come and toss the *pila* with me; — that is," she added, with mock reverence, "if so grand a person as the prefect of Rome can play at ball!"

"And why not, my Annia," asked her mother, proudly; "even the world-ruling Julius loved his game of ball."

"Ah, but our Marcus is greater than the great Cæsar. Is he not, mother?" Annia asked, teasingly.

"Aye, that he is," the mother answered, feelingly; "for, know that he has this day given up to thee, his sister, one half of his heritage, and more — unwise and improvident youth!" she added, fondly.

"So let it end, mother," the boy said, as the pretty Annia sprang to him with a caress. "Come, Annia, let us see who can toss the *pila* best — a woman of property, such as thou, or the prefect of three days." And as hand in hand the brother and sister passed cheerily through the pillared portico, the mother looked after them with a happy heart and said, as did that earlier noble Roman matron of whom history tells us: "*These* are my jewels!"

Annia, The Sister Of Marcus, And Her Pets.

The days passed. Winter grew to spring. The ides of March have come. And now it is one of the spring holidays of Rome, the fourteenth of March in the year 138 — the *Equiria*, or festival of Mars. Rome is astir early, and every street of the great city is thronged with citizens and strangers, slaves and soldiers, all hurrying toward the great pleasure-ground of Rome — the Circus Maximus. Through every portal the crowds press into the vast building, filling its circular seats, anxious for the spectacle. For the magistrate of the games for this day, it is said, is to be the young Marcus Annius, he who was prefect of the city during the last Latin Games; and, more than this, the festival is to close with a grand *venatio* — a wild-beast hunt!

There is a stir of expectation; a burst of trumpets from the Capitol; and all along the Sacred Street and through the crowded Forum goes up the shout, "Here they come!" With the flutes playing merrily, with swaying standards and sacred statues gleaming in silver and gold, with proud young cadets on horse and on foot, with priests in their robes and guards with crested helms, with strange and marvellous beasts led by burly keepers, with a long string of skilled performers, restless horses, and gleaming chariots, through the Forum and down the Sacred Street winds the long procession, led by the boy magistrate, Marcus of Rome, the favorite of the Emperor. A golden chaplet, wrought in crusted leaves, circles his head; a purple *toga* drapes his trim, young figure; while the flutes and trumpets play their loudest before him, and the stout guards march at the heels of his bright-bay pony. So into the great circus passes the long procession, and as it files into the arena, two hundred thousand excited people — think, boys, of a circus-tent that holds two hundred thousand people! — rise to their feet and welcome it with hearty hand-clapping. The trumpets sound the prelude, the young magistrate (standing in his *suggestus*, or state box) flings the *mappa*, or white flag, into the course as the signal for the start; and, as a ringing shout goes up, four glittering chariots, rich in their decorations of gold and polished ivory, and each drawn by four plunging horses, burst from their arched stalls and dash around the track. Green, blue, red, white — the colors of the drivers stream from their tunics. Around and around they go. Now one and now another is ahead. The people strain and cheer, and many a wager is laid as to the victor. Another shout! The red chariot, turning too sharply, grates against the *meta*, or short pillar that stands at the upper end of the track, guarding the low central wall; the horses rear and plunge, the driver struggles manfully to control them, but all in vain; over goes the chariot, while the now maddened horses dash wildly on until checked by mounted attendants and led off to their stalls.

"Blue! blue!" "Green! green!" rise the varying shouts, as the contending chariots still struggle for the lead. White is far behind. Now comes the seventh or final round. Blue leads! No, green is ahead! Down the home stretch they go in a magnificent dash, neck and neck, and then the cheer of victory is heard, as, with a final spurt the green rider strikes the white cord first and the race is won!

And there, where the race is fiercest and the excitement most intense, sits the staid young Marcus, unmoved, unexcited, busy with his ivory tablets and his own high thoughts! For this wise young Stoic, true to his accepted philosophy, had mastered even the love of excitement — think of that, you circus-loving boys! He has left it on record that, even as a youth, he had learned "to be neither of the green nor of the blue party at the games in the circus," and while he looked upon such shows as dangerous and wasteful (for in those days they cost the state immense sums), he felt, still, that the people enjoyed them, and he said simply: "We cannot make men as we would have them; we must bear with them as they are and make the best of them we can." And so it happened that at this splendid race at which, to please the people, he presided as magistrate, this boy of sixteen sat probably the only unmoved spectator in that whole vast amphitheatre.

Now, in the interval between the races, come the athletic sports; foot-racing and wrestling, rope-dancing and high leaping, quoit-throwing and javelin matches. One man runs a race with a fleet Cappadocian horse; another expert rider drives two bare-backed horses twice around the track, leaping from back to back as the horses dash around. Can you see any very great difference between the circus performance of A. D. 138 and one of A. D. 1886?

Among the throng of "artistes" on that far-off March day there came a bright little fellow of ten or eleven years, a rope-dancer and a favorite with the crowd. Light and agile, he trips along the slender rope that stretches high above the arena. Right before the magistrate's box the boy poises in mid air, and even the thoughtful young director of the games looks up at the graceful motions of the boy. Hark! a warning shout goes up; now, another;

the poor little rope-dancer, anxious to find favor in the eyes of the young noble, over-exerts himself, loses his balance on the dizzy rope, and, toppling over, falls with a cruel thud to the ground, and lies there before the great state box with a broken neck — dead. Marcus hears the shout, he sees the falling boy. Vaulting from his canopied box he leaps down into the arena, and so tender is he of others, Stoic though he be, that he has the poor rope-dancer's head in his lap even before the attendants can reach him. But no life remains in that bruised little body, and, as Marcus tenderly resigns the dead gymnast to the less sympathetic slaves, he commands that ever after a bed shall be laid beneath the rope as a protection against such fatal falls. This became the rule; and, when next you see the safety-net spread beneath the rope-walkers, the trapeze performers, and those who perform similar "terrific" feats, remember that its use dates back to the humane order of Marcus, the boy magistrate, seventeen centuries ago.

But, in those old days, the people had to be amused — whatever happened. Human life was held too cheaply for a whole festival to be stopped because a little boy was killed, and so the sports went on. Athletes and gymnasts did their best to excel; amidst wild excitement the chariots whirled around and around the course, and then the arena was cleared for the final act — the wild beast hunt.

The wary keepers raise the stout gratings before the dens and cages, and the wild animals, freed from their prisons, rush into the great open space, blink stupidly in the glaring light, and then with roar and growl echo the shouts of the spectators. Here are great lions from Numidia and tigers from far Arabia, wolves from the Apennines and bears from Libya, not caged and half-tamed as we see them now, but wild and fierce, loose in the arena. Now the hunters swarm in, on horse and on foot, — trained and supple Thracian gladiators, skilled Gætulian hunters, with archers, and spearmen, and net-throwers. All around the great arena rages the cruel fight. Here, a lion stands at bay; there, a tigress crouches for the spring; a snarling wolf snaps at a keen-eyed Thracian, or a bear with ungainly trot shambles away from the spear of his persecutor. Eager and watchful the hunters shoot and thrust, while the vast audience, more eager, more relentless, more brutal than beast or hunter, applaud and shout and cheer. But the young magistrate, who had, through all his life, a marked distaste for such cruel sport, turns from the arena, and, again taking out his tablets, busies himself with his writing, unmoved by the contest and carnage before him.

The last hunted beast lies dead in the arena; the last valorous hunter has been honored with his *palma*, or reward, as victor; the slaves stand ready with hook and rope to drag off the slaughtered animals; the great crowd pours out of the vast three-storied building; the shops in the porticos are noisy with the talk of buyers and sellers; the boy magistrate and his escort pass through the waiting throng; and the Festival Games are over. But, ere young Marcus reaches the Forum on his return, a shout goes up from the people, and, just before the beautiful temple of the Twin Gods, Castor and Pollux, where the throng is densest, flowers and wreaths are thrown beneath his pony's feet, and a storm of voices raises the shout:

"*Ave Imperator! Ave Cæsar!*"

"What means that shout, Aufidius?" he asked his friend, who rode in the escort. But the only reply Aufidius made was to join his voice with that of the enthusiastic throng in a second shout; "*Ave Imperator! Auguste, Dii te servent!*" (Hail, O Emperor! The gods save your majesty!)

Then Marcus knew that the decree of the dying Emperor Hadrian had been confirmed, and that he, Marcus Annius Verus, the descendant of the ancient kings, the boy philosopher, the unassuming son of a noble mother, had been adopted as the son and successor of his uncle Antoninus, who was to reign after Hadrian's death, and that where he went, through the Forum and up the Sacred Street, there rode the heir to the greatest throne in the world, the future Emperor of Rome.

A Stoic still, unmoved, save for the slight flush that tinged his cheek as he acknowledged the greeting of the happy people, he passed on to his mother's house, and, in that dear home, amid the green gardens of the Cœlian Hill, he heard her lips speak her congratulations, and bent his head to receive her kiss of blessing.

"I lose a son, but gain an emperor," she said.

"No, my mother," the boy replied, proudly, "me thou shalt never lose. For, though I leave this dear home for the palace of the Cæsars, my heart is still here with that noble mother from whom I learned lessons of piety and benevolence and simplicity of life, and abstinence from evil deeds and evil thoughts."

Before five months had passed the great Emperor Hadrian died at Baiæ, in his hill-shaded palace by the sea, and the wise, country-loving uncle of Marcus succeeded to the throne as the Emperor Antoninus Pius. During all his glorious reign of twenty-three years, he had no more devoted admirer, subject, helper, and friend, than his adopted son and acknowledged successor, Marcus, who, in the year A. D. 161, ascended the throne of the Cæsars as the great Emperor Marcus Aurelius Antoninus.

The life of this Roman Marcus was one of unsought honors and titles. At six, a knight of the Equestrian Order; at eight, one of the priests of Mars; at twelve, a rigid Stoic; at sixteen, a magistrate of the city; at seventeen, a quæstor, or revenue officer; at nineteen, a consul and Cæsar; at forty, an emperor, — he was always clear-headed and clean-hearted, beloved by his people and honored by all, making this one rule the guide of all his actions: "Every moment think steadily as a Roman and a man, to do what thou hast in hand with perfect and simple dignity, with affection and freedom and justice."

A noble boy; a noble man; preserving, as has been said of him, "in a time of universal corruption, a nature sweet, pure, self-denying, and unaffected," — he teaches us all, boys and men alike, a lesson of real manliness. Here are two of his precepts, which we are none of us too young to remember, none of us too old to forget: "The best way of avenging thyself is not to become like the wrong-doer"; "Let me offer to the gods the best that is in me; so shall I be a strong man, ripened by age, a friend of the public good, a Roman, an emperor, a soldier at his post awaiting the signal of his trumpet, a man ready to quit life without a fear." The foremost boy of his time, manly, modest, princely, brave, and true, we can surely find no more fitting representative with which to open this series of "Historic Boys" than the boy magistrate, Marcus of Rome, the greatest and best of the Antonines.

FOOTNOTES:

[1] *Præfectus urbi*: governor of the city.

[2] Not true, but *most* true.

[3] An officer of the treasury.

[4] Armed police.

II. BRIAN OF MUNSTER: THE BOY CHIEFTAIN.

(Afterward Brian Boru, King of Ireland.) A.D. 948.

Into that picturesque and legend-filled section of Ireland now known as the County Clare, where over rocks and boulders the Shannon, "noblest of Irish rivers," rushes down past Killaloe and Castle Connell to Limerick and the sea, there rode one fair summer morning, many, many years ago, a young Irish lad. The skirt of his parti-colored *lenn*, or kilt, was richly embroidered and fringed with gold; his *inar*, or jacket, close-fitting and silver-trimmed, was open at the throat, displaying the embroidered *lenn* and the *torc*, or twisted collar of gold about his sturdy neck, while a purple scarf, held the jacket at the waist. A gleaming, golden brooch secured the long plaid *brat*, or shawl, that dropped from his left shoulder; broad bracelets encircled his bare and curiously tattooed arms, and from an odd-looking golden spiral at the back of his head his thick and dark-red hair fell in flowing ringlets upon his broad shoulders. Raw-hide shoes covered his feet, and his bronze shield and short war-ax hung conveniently from his saddle of skins. A strong guard of pikemen and gallowglasses, or heavy-armed footmen, followed at his pony's heels, and seemed an escort worthy a king's son.

A strong-limbed, cleanly-built lad of fifteen was this sturdy young horseman, who now rode down to the Ath na Borumma, or Ford of the Tribute, just above the rapids of the Shannon, near the town of Killaloe. And as he reined in his pony, he turned and bade his herald, Cogoran, sound the trumpet-blast that should announce to the Clan of Cas the return, from his years of foster-age, of the young *flaith*, or chieftain, Brian, the son of Kennedy, King of Thomond.

But ere the strong-lunged Cogoran could wind his horn, the hearts of all the company grew numb with fear as across the water the low, clear strains of a warning-song sounded from the haunted gray-stone, — the mystic rock of Carrick-lee, that overhung the tumbling rapids:

"Never yet for fear of foe,

By the ford of Killaloe,
Stooped the crests of heroes free —
Sons of Cas by Carrick-lee.

"Falls the arm that smites the foe,
By the ford of Killaloe;
Chilled the heart that boundeth free,
By the rock of Carrick-lee.

"He who knows not fear of foe,
Fears the ford of Killaloe;
Fears the voice that chants his dree,
From the rock of Carrick-lee."

Young Brian was full of the superstition of his day — superstition that even yet lives amid the simple peasantry of Ireland, and peoples rocks, and woods, and streams with good and evil spirits, fairies, sprites, and banshees; and no real, native Irish lad could fail to tremble before the mysterious song. Sorely troubled, he turned to Cogoran inquiringly, and that faithful retainer said in a rather shaky voice:

"'T is your warning-song, O noble young chief! 't is the voice of the banshee of our clan — *A-oib-hinn*, the wraith of Carrick-lee."

Just then from behind the haunted gray-rock a fair young girl appeared, tripping lightly across the large stepping-stones that furnished the only means of crossing the ford of Killaloe.

"See — see!" said Cogoran, grasping his young lord's arm; "she comes for thee. 'T is thy doom, O Master — the fiend of Carrick-lee!"

"So fair a fiend should bring me naught of grief," said young Brian, stoutly enough, though it must be confessed his heart beat fast and loud. "O Spirit of the Waters!" he exclaimed; "O banshee of Clan Cas! why thus early in his life dost thou come to summon the son of Kennedy the King?"

The young girl turned startled eyes upon the group of armed and warlike men, and grasping the skirt of her white and purple *lenn*, turned as if to flee, — when Cogoran, with a loud laugh, cried out:

"Now, fool and double fool am I, — fit brother to Sitric the blind, the black King of Dublin! Why, 't is no banshee, O noble young chief, 't is but thy foster-sister, Eimer, the daughter of Conor, Eimer the golden-haired!"

"Nay, is it so? St. Senanus be praised!" said Brian, greatly relieved. "Cross to us, maiden; cross to us," he said. "Fear nothing; 't is but Brian, thy foster-brother, returning to his father's home."

The girl swiftly crossed the ford and bowed her golden head in a vassal's welcome to the young lord.

"Welcome home, O brother," she said. "Even now, my lord, thy father awaits the sound of thy horn as he sits in the great seat beneath his kingly shield. And I — — "

"And thou, maiden," sad Brian, gayly, "thou must needs lurk behind the haunted rock of Carrick-lee, to freeze the heart of young Brian at his home-coming, with thy banshee song."

Eimer of the golden hair laughed a ringing laugh. "Say'st thou so, brother?" she said. "Does the 'Scourge of the Danes' shrink thus at a maiden's voice?"

"Who calls me the 'Scourge of the Danes'?" asked Brian.

"So across the border do they say that the maidens of King Callaghan's court call the boy Brian, the son of Kennedy," the girl made answer.

"Who faces the Danes, my sister, faces no tender foe," said Brian, "and the court of the King of Cashel is no ladies' hall in these hard-striking times. But wind thy horn, Cogoran, and cross we the ford to greet the king, my father."

Loud and clear the herald's call rose above the rush of the rapids, and as the boy and his followers crossed the ford, the gates of the palace, or *dun*, of King Kennedy of Thomond were flung open, and the band of welcomers, headed by Mahon, Brian's eldest brother, rode out to greet the lad.

Nine hundred years ago the tribe of Cas was one of the most powerful of the many Irish clans. The whole of Thomond, or North Munster, was under their sway, and from them, say the old records, "it was never lawful to levy rent, or tribute, or pledge, or hostage, or fostership fees," so strong and free were they. When the clans of Munster gathered for battle, it was the right of the Clan of Cas to lead in the attack, and to guard the rear when returning from any invasion. It gave kings to the throne of Munster, and valiant leaders in warfare with the Danes, who, in the tenth century, poured their hosts into Ireland, conquering and destroying. In the year 948, in which our sketch opens, the head of this powerful clan was Cennedigh, or Kennedy, King of Thomond. His son Brian had, in accordance with an old Irish custom, passed his boyhood in "fosterage" at the court of Callaghan, King of Cashel, in East Munster. Brought up amid warlike scenes, where battles with the Danish invaders were of frequent occurrence, young Brian had now, at fifteen, completed the years of his fostership, and was a lad of strong and dauntless courage, cool and clear-headed, and a firm foe of Ireland's scourge — the fierce "Dub-Gaile," or "Black Gentiles," as the Danes were called.

The feast of welcome was over. The bards had sung their heroic songs to the accompaniment of the *cruot*, or harp; the fool had played his pranks, and the juggler his tricks, and the chief bard, who was expected to be familiar with "more than seven times fifty stories, great and small," had given the best from his list; and as they sat thus in the *cuirmtech*, or great hall, of the long, low-roofed house of hewn oak that scarcely rose above the stout earthen ramparts that defended it, swift messengers came bearing news of a great gathering of Danes for the ravaging of Munster, and the especial plundering of the Clan of Cas.

"Thou hast come in right fitting time, O son!" said Kennedy the King. "Here is need of strong arms and stout hearts. How say ye, noble lords and worthy chieftains? Dare we face in fight this, so great a host?"

But as chiefs and counsellors were discussing the king's question, advising fight or flight as they deemed wisest, young Brian sprung into the assembly, war-ax in hand.

"What, fathers of Clan Cas," he cried, all aflame with excitement, "will ye stoop to parley with hard-hearted pirates — ye, who never brooked injustice or tyranny from any king of all the kings of Erin — ye, who never yielded even the leveret of a hare in tribute to Leinsterman or Dane? 'T is for the Clan of Cas to demand tribute, — not to pay it! Summon our vassals to war. Place me, O King, my father, here at the Ford of the Tribute and bid me make test of the lessons of my fostership. Know ye not how the boy champion, Cuchullin of Ulster, held the ford for five long days against all the hosts of Connaught? What boy hath done, boy may do. Death can come but once!"

The lad's impetuous words fired the whole assembly, the gillies and retainers caught up the cry, and, with the wild enthusiasm that has marked the quick-hearted Irishman from Brian's day to this, "they all," so says the record, "kissed the ground and gave a terrible shout." Beacon fires blazed from cairn and hill-top, and from "the four points" — from north and south and east and west, came the men of Thomond rallying around their chieftains on the banks of Shannon.

With terrible ferocity the Danish hosts fell upon Ireland. From Dublin to Cork the coast swarmed with their war-ships and the land echoed the tramp of their swordsmen. Across the fair fields of Meath and Tipperary, "the smooth-plained grassy land of Erinn," from Shannon to the sea, the kings and chieftains of Ireland gathered to withstand the shock of the invaders. Their chief blow was struck at "Broccan's Brake" in the County Meath, and "on that field," says the old Irish record, "fell the kings and chieftains, the heirs to the crown, and the royal princes of Erinn." There fell Kennedy the King and two of his stalwart sons. But at the Ford of the Tribute, Brian, the boy chieftain, kept his post and hurled back again and again the Danes of Limerick as they swarmed up the valley of the Shannon to support their countrymen on the plains of Meath.

The haunted gray-stone of Carrick-lee, from which Brian had heard the song of the supposed banshee, rose sharp and bold above the rushing waters; and against it and around it Brian and his followers stood at bay, battling against the Danish hosts. "Ill-luck was it for the foreigner," says the record, "when that youth was born — Brian, the son of Kennedy." In the very midst of the stubborn fight at the ford, and around from a jutting point of the rock of Carrick-lee, a light shallop came speeding down the rapids. In the prow stood a female figure, all in white, from the gleaming golden *lann*, or crescent, that held her flowing veil, to the hem of her gracefully falling *lenn*, or robe. And above the din of the strife a clear voice sang:

"First to face the foreign foe,
First to strike the battle blow;
Last to turn from triumph back,
Last to leave the battle's wrack;
Clan of Cas shall victors be
When they fight at Carrick-lee."

It was, of course, only the brave young Eimer of the golden hair bringing fresh arms in her shallop to Brian and his fighting-men; but as the sun, bursting through the clouds, flashed full upon the shining war-ax which she held aloft, the superstitious Danes saw in the floating figure the "White Lady of the Rapids," the banshee, *A-oib-hinn*, the fairy guardian of the Clan of Cas. Believing, therefore, that they could not prevail against her powerful aid, they turned and fled in dismay from the flowing river and the haunted rock.

But fast upon young Brian's victory came the tearful news of the battle of Broccan's Brake and the defeat of the Irish kings. Of all the brave lad's family only his eldest brother Mahon escaped from that fatal field; and now he reigned in place of Kennedy, his father, as King of Thomond. But the victorious Danes overran all Southern Ireland, and the brothers Mahon and Brian found that they could not successfully face in open field the hosts of their invaders. So these two "stout, able, valiant pillars," these two "fierce, lacerating, magnificent heroes," as the brothers are called in the curious and wordy old Irish record, left their mud-walled fortress-palace by the Shannon, and with "all their people and all their chattels" went deep into the forests of Cratloe and the rocky fastnesses of the County Clare; and there they lived the life of robber chieftains, harassing and plundering the Danes of Limerick and their recreant Irish allies, and guarding against frequent surprise and attack. But so hazardous and unsettled a life was terribly exhausting, and "at length each party of them became tired of the other," and finally King Mahon made peace with the Danes of Limerick.

But "Brian the brave" would make no truce with a hated foe. "Tell my brother," he said, when messengers brought him word of Mahon's treaty, "that Brian, the son of Kennedy, knows no peace with foreign invaders. Though all others yield and are silent, yet will I never!"

And with this defiance the boy chieftain and "the young champions of the tribe of Cas" went deeper into the woods and fastnesses of the County Clare, and for months kept up a fierce guerilla warfare. The Danish tyrants knew neither peace nor rest from his swift and sudden attacks. Much booty of "satins and silken cloths, both scarlet and green, pleasing jewels and saddles beautiful and foreign" did they lose to this active young chieftain, and much tribute of cows and hogs and other possessions did he force from them. So dauntless an outlaw did he become that his name struck terror from Galway Bay to the banks of Shannon, and from Lough Derg to the Burren of Clare. "When he inflicted not evil on the foreigners in the day," the quaint old record asserts, "he was sure to do it in the next night, and when he did it not in the night he was sure to do it in the following day."

To many an adventurous boy the free outlaw life of this daring lad of nine centuries ago may seem alluring. But "life in the greenwood" had little romance for such old-time outlaws as Brian Boru and Robin Hood and their imitators. To them it was stern reality, and meant constant struggle and vigilance. They were outcasts and Ishmaels — "their hands against every man and every man's hand against them," — and though the pleasant summer weather brought many sunshiny days and starlit nights, the cold, damp, and dismal days took all the poetry out of this roving life, and sodden forests and relentless foes brought dreary and disheartening hours. Trust me, boys, this so-called "free and jolly life of the bold outlaw," which so many story-papers picture, whether it be with Brian Boru in distant Ireland, nine hundred years ago, or in Sherwood Forest with Robin Hood, or with some "Buckeye Jim" on our own Montana hill-sides to-day, is not "what it is cracked up to be." Its attractiveness is found solely in those untruthful tales that give you only the little that seems to be sweet, but say nothing of the much that is so very, very harsh and bitter. Month by month the boy chieftain strove against fearful odds, day by day he saw his brave band grow less and less, dying under the unpitying swords of the Danes and the hardships of this wandering life, until of all the high-spirited and valiant comrades that had followed him into the hills of Clare only fifteen remained.

One chill April day, as Brian sat alone before the gloomy cave that had given him a winter shelter in the depths of the forests of Clare, his quick ear, well trained in wood-craft, caught the sound of a light step in the thicket. Snatching his ever-ready spear, he stood on guard and demanded:

"Who is there?"

No answer followed his summons. But as he waited and listened, he heard the notes of a song, low and gentle, as if for his ear alone:

"Chieftain of the stainless shield,
Prince who brooks no tribute fee;
Ne'er shall he to pagan yield
Who prevailed at Carrick-lee.
Rouse thee, arm thee, hark and heed,
Erin's strength in Erin's need."

"'T is the banshee," was the youth's first thought. "The guardian of our clan urgeth me to speedier action." And then he called aloud: "Who sings of triumph to Brian the heavy-hearted?"

"Be no longer Brian the heavy-hearted; be, as thou ever art, Brian the brave!" came the reply, and through the parting thicket appeared, not the dreaded vision of *A-oib-hinn*, the banshee, but the fair young face of his foster-sister, Eimer of the golden hair.

"Better days await thee, Brian, my brother," she said; "Mahon the King bids thee meet him at Holy Isle. None dared bring his message for fear of the death-dealing Danes who have circled thee with their earth-lines. But what dare not I do for so gallant a foster-brother?"

With the courtesy that marked the men of even those savage times, the boy chieftain knelt and kissed the hem of the daring little maiden's purple robe.

"And what wishes my brother, the king, O Eimer of the golden hair?" he said. "Knows he not that Brian has sworn never to bend his neck to the foreigner?"

"That does he know right well," replied the girl. "But his only words to me were: 'Bid Brian my brother take heart and keep this tryst with me, and the sons of Kennedy may still stand, unfettered, kings of Erin.'"

"The Boy Chieftain Knelt And Kissed The Hem Of The Darling Little Maiden's Purple Robe."

So Brian kept the tryst; and where, near the southern shores of Lough Derg, the Holy Isle still lies all strewn with the ruins of the seven churches that gave it this name, the outlawed young chieftain met the king. Braving the dangers of Danish capture and death, he had come unattended to meet his brother.

"Where, O Brian, are thy followers?" King Mahon inquired.

"Save the fifteen faithful men that remain to me in the caves of Uim-Bloit," said the lad, "the bones of my followers rest on many a field from the mountains of Connaught to the gates of

Limerick; for their chieftain, O my brother, maketh no truce with the foe."

"Thou art but a boy, O Brian, and like a boy thou dost talk," said the king, reprovingly. "Thy pride doth make thee imprudent. For what hast thou gained, since, spite of all, thy followers lie dead!"

"Gained!" exclaimed the young chieftain, impetuously, as he faced Mahon the King; "I have gained the right to be called true son of the Clan of Cas — of ancestors who would brook no insult, who would pay no tribute fee to invaders, who would give no hostage; and as to my trusty liegemen who have fallen — is it not the inheritance of the Clan of Cas to die for their honor and their homes?" demanded Brian. "So surely it is no honor in valorous men, my brother, to abandon without battle or conflict their father's inheritance to Danes and traitorous kings!"

The unyielding courage of the lad roused the elder brother to action, and, secretly, but swiftly, he gathered the chiefs of the clan for council in the *dun* of King Mahon by the ford of Killaloe. "Freedom for Erin and death to the Danes!" cried they — "as the voice of one man," says the record. Again the warning beacons flamed from cairn and hill-top. In the shadow of the "Rock of Cashel," the royal sun-burst, the banner of the ancient kings, was flung to the breeze, and clansmen and vassals and allies rallied beneath its folds to strike one mighty blow for the redemption of Ireland.

In the county of Tipperary, in the midst of what is called "the golden valley," this remarkable "Rock of Cashel" looms up three hundred feet above the surrounding plain, its top, even now, crowned with the ruins of what were in Brian's day palace and chapel, turret and battlement and ancient tower. Beneath the rough archway of the triple ramparts at the foot of the rock, and up the sharp ascent, there rode one day the herald of Ivar, the Danish King of Limerick. Through the gate-way of the palace he passed, and striding into the audience-hall, spoke thus to Mahon the King:

"Hear, now, O King! Ivar, the son of Sitric, King of Limerick and sole Over-lord of Munster, doth summon thee, his vassal, to give up to him this fortress of Cashel, to disperse thy followers, to send to him at Limerick, bounden with chains, the body of Brian the outlaw, and to render unto him tribute and hostage."

King Mahon glanced proudly out to where upon the ramparts fluttered the flag of Ireland.

"Say to Ivar, the son of Sitric," he said, "that Mahon, King of Thomond, spurns his summons, and will pay no tribute for his own inheritance."

"And say thou too," cried his impetuous younger brother, "that Brian, the son of Kennedy, and all the men of the Clan of Cas prefer destruction and death rather than submit to the tyranny of pirates and the over-lordship of foreigners and Danes!"

"Hear then, Mahon, King of Thomond; hear thou and all thy clan, the words of Ivar, the son of Sitric," came the stern warning of the Danish herald. "Thus says the king: I will gather against thee a greater muster and hosting, and I will so ravage and destroy the Clan of Cas that there shall not be left of ye one man to guide a horse's head across a ford, an abbot or a venerable person within the four corners of Munster who shall not be utterly destroyed or brought under subjection to me, Ivar the king!"

"Tell thy master," said Mahon the King, unmoved by this terrible threat, "that the Clan of Cas defy his boastful words, and will show in battle which are lords of Erin."

"And tell thy master," said his brother, "that Brian the outlaw will come to Limerick not bound with chains, but to bind them."

The Danish power was strong and terrible, but the action of the two valiant brothers was swift and their example was inspiring. Clansmen and vassals flocked to their standard, and a great and warlike host gathered in old Cashel. Brian led them to battle, and near a willow forest, close to the present town of Tipperary, the opposing forces met in a battle that lasted "from sunrise to mid-day." And the sun-burst banner of the ancient kings streamed victorious over a conquered field, and the hosts of the Danes were routed. From Tipperary to Limerick, Brian pursued the flying enemy; and capturing Limerick, took therefrom great stores of booty and many prisoners; and the queer old Irish record thus briefly tells the terrible story of young Brian's vengeance — a story that fittingly shows us the cruel customs of those savage days of old, days now fortunately gone for ever: "The fort and the good town he reduced to a cloud of smoke and to red fire afterward. The whole of the captives were collected on the hills of Saingel, and every one that was fit for war was killed, and every one that was fit for a slave was enslaved."

And from the day of Limerick's downfall the star of Ireland brightened, as in battle after battle, Brian Boru, [5] the wise and valiant young chieftain, was hailed as victor and deliverer from sea to sea.

But now he is a lad no longer, and the story of the boy chieftain gives place to the record of the valiant soldier and the able king. For upon the death of his brother Mahon, in the year 976, Brian became King of Thomond, of Munster, and Cashel. Then uniting the rival clans and tribes under his sovereign rule, he was crowned at Tara, in the year 1000, "Ard-righ," or "High King of Erinn." The reign of this great king of Ireland was peaceful and prosperous. He built churches, fostered learning, made bridges and causeways, and constructed a road around the coast of the whole kingdom. In his palace at Kincora, near the old *dun* of his father, King Kennedy, by the ford of Killaloe, he "dispensed a royal hospitality, administered a rigid and impartial justice, and so continued in prosperity for the rest of his reign, having been at his death thirty-eight years King of Munster and fifteen years Sovereign of all Ireland."

So the boy chieftain came to be King of Ireland, and the story of his death is as full of interest and glory as the record of his boyish deeds. For Brian grew to be an old, old man, and the Danes and some of the restless Irishmen whom he had brought under his sway revolted against his rule. So the "grand old king of ninety years" led his armies out from the tree-shaded ramparts of royal Kincora, and meeting the enemy on the plains of Dublin, fought on Friday, April 23, 1014, near the little fishing station of Clontarf, the "last and most terrible struggle of Northman and

Gael, of Pagan and Christian, on Irish soil." It was a bloody day for Ireland; but though the aged king and four of his six sons, with eleven thousand of his followers were slain on that fatal field, the Danes were utterly routed, and the battle of Clontarf freed Ireland forever from their invasions and tyrannies.

"Remember the glories of Brian the brave,
Though the days of the hero are o'er;
Though lost to Mononia and cold in the grave,
He returns to Kincora no more!
That star of the field, which so often has poured
Its beam on the battle, is set;
But enough of its glory remains on each sword
To light us to victory yet!"

So sings Thomas Moore in one of his inspiring "Irish Melodies"; and when hereafter you hear or read of Brian Boru, remember him not only as Ireland's greatest king, but also as the dauntless lad who held the ford at Killaloe, and preferred the privations of an outlaw's life to a disgraceful peace; and who, dying an old, old man, still kept his love of country undiminished, and sealed with his blood the liberty of his native land, declaring, as the poet Moore puts it in his glowing verse:

"No, Freedom! whose smiles we shall never resign,
Go tell our invaders, the Danes,
That 't is sweeter to bleed for an age at thy shrines
Than to sleep but a moment in chains!"

Kincora, the royal home of Brian the King, is now so lost in ruins that travellers cannot tell the throne-room from the cowhouse; Cashel's high rock is deserted and dismantled; and on the hill of Tara the palace of the ancient Irish kings is but a grassgrown mound. But, though palaces crumble and nations decay, the remembrance of truth and valor and glowing patriotism lives on forever, and to the boys and girls of this more favored time the stories of noble lives and glorious deeds come as a priceless legacy, bidding them be stout-hearted in the face of danger and strong-souled in spite of temptation. So to every lover of daring deeds and loyal lives time cannot dim the shining record of the great King of Ireland, Brian Boru — Brian of Munster: the Boy Chieftain.

FOOTNOTES:

[5] *Boru*, or *Borumha*, the tribute; therefore "Brian of the Tribute."

III. OLAF OF NORWAY: THE BOY VIKING.

(Afterward King Olaf II., of Norway — "St. Olaf.")
A.D. 1010.

Old Rane, the helmsman, whose fierce mustaches and shaggy shoulder-mantle made him look like some grim old northern wolf, held high in air the great bison-horn filled with foaming mead.

"Skoal to the Viking! Hael; was-hael!" [6] rose his exultant shout. From a hundred sturdy throats the cry re-echoed till the vaulted hall of the Swedemen's conquered castle rang again.

"Skoal to the Viking! Hael; was-hael!" and in the centre of that throng of mail-clad men and tossing spears, standing firm and fearless upon the interlocked and uplifted shields of three stalwart fighting-men, a stout-limbed lad of scarce thirteen, with flowing light-brown hair and flushed and eager face, brandished his sword vigorously in acknowledgment of the jubilant shout that rang again through the dark and smoke-stained hall, "Was-hael to the sea-wolf's son! Skoal to Olaf the King!"

Then above of the din and clash of shouting and of steel rose the voice of Sigvat the saga-man, or song-man of the young viking, singing loud and sturdily:

"Olaf the King is on his cruise,
His blue steel staining,
Rich booty gaining,
And all men trembling at the news.
Up, war-wolf's brood! our young fir's name
O'ertops the forest trees in fame,
Our stout young Olaf knows no fear.
Though fell the fray,
He's blithe and gay,
And warriors fall beneath his spear.
Who can't defend the wealth they have
Must die or share with the rover brave!"

A fierce and warlike song, boys and girls, to raise in honor of so young a lad. But those were fierce and warlike days when men were stirred by the recital of bold and daring deeds — those old, old days, eight hundred years ago, when Olaf, the boy viking, the pirate chief of a hundred mail-clad men, stood upon the uplifted shields of his exultant fighting-men in the grim and smoke-stained hall of the gray castle of captured Sigtun, oldest of Swedish cities.

Take your atlas, and, turning to the map of Sweden, place your finger on the city of Stockholm. Do you notice that it lies at the easterly end of a large lake? That is the Maelar, beautiful with winding channels, pine-covered islands, and rocky shores. It is peaceful and quiet now, and palace and villa and quaint northern farm-house stand unmolested on its picturesque borders. But channels, and islands, and rocky shores have echoed and re-echoed with the war-shouts of many a fierce sea-rover since those far-off days when Olaf, the boy viking, and his Norwegian ships of war plowed through the narrow sea-strait, and ravaged the fair shores of the Maelar with fire and sword.

Stockholm, the "Venice of the North," as it is called, was not then in existence; and little now remains of old Sigtun save ruined walls. But travellers may still see the three tall towers of the ancient town, and the great stone-heap, alongside which young Olaf drew his ships of war, and over which his pirate crew swarmed into Sigtun town, and planted the victorious banner of the golden serpent upon the conquered walls.

For this fair young Olaf came of hardy Norse stock. His father, Harald Graenske, or "Greymantle," one of the tributary kings of Norway, had fallen a victim to the tortures of the haughty Swedish queen; and now his son, a boy of scarce thirteen, but a warrior already by training and from desire, came to avenge his father's death. His mother, the Queen Aasta, equipped a large dragon-ship or war-vessel for her adventurous son, and with the lad, as helmsman and guardian, was sent old Rane, whom men called "the far-travelled," because he had sailed westward as far as England and southward to Nörvasund (by which name men then knew the Straits of Gibraltar). Boys toughened quickly in those stirring days, and this lad, who, because he was commander of a dragon-ship, was called Olaf the King — though he had no land to rule, — was of viking blood, and quickly learned the trade of war. Already, among the rocks and sands of Sodermann, upon the Swedish coast, he had won his first battle over a superior force of Danish war-vessels.

Other ships of war joined him; the name of Olaf the Brave was given him by right of daring deeds, and "Skoal to the Viking!" rang from the sturdy throats of his followers as the little sea-king of thirteen was lifted in triumph upon the battle-dented shields.

But a swift runner bursts into the gray hall of Sigtun. "To your ships, O King; to your ships!" he cries. "Olaf, the Swedish king, men say, is planting a forest of spears along the sea-strait, and, except ye push out now, ye may not get out at all!"

The nimble young chief sprang from the upraised shields.

"To your ships, vikings, all!" he shouted. "Show your teeth, war-wolves! Up with the serpent banner, and death to Olaf the Swede!"

Straight across the lake to the sea-strait, near where Stockholm now stands, the vikings sailed, young Olaf's dragon-ship taking the lead. But all too late; for, across the narrow strait, the Swedish king had stretched great chains, and had filled up the channel with stocks and stones. Olaf and his Norsemen were fairly trapped; the Swedish spears waved in wild and joyful triumph, and King Olaf, the Swede, said with grim satisfaction to his lords: "See, jarls and lendermen, the Fat Boy is caged at last!" For he never spoke of his stout young Norwegian namesake and rival save as "Olaf Tjocke," — Olaf the Thick, or Fat.

The boy viking stood by his dragon-headed prow, and shook his clenched fist at the obstructed sea-strait and the Swedish spears.

"Shall we, then, land, Rane, and fight our way through?" he asked.

"Fight our way through?" said old Rane, who had been in

many another tight place in his years of sea-roving, but none so close as this. "Why, King, they be a hundred to one!"

"And if they be, what then?" said impetuous Olaf. "Better fall as a viking breaking Swedish spears, than die a straw-death [7] as Olaf of Sweden's bonder-man. May we not cut through these chains?"

"As soon think of cutting the solid earth, King," said the helmsman.

"So; and why not, then?" young Olaf exclaimed, struck with a brilliant idea. "Ho, Sigvat," he said, turning to his saga-man, "what was that lowland under the cliff where thou didst say the pagan Upsal king was hanged in his own golden chains by his Finnish queen?"

"'T is called the fen of Agnefit, O King," replied the saga-man, pointing toward where it lay.

"Why, then, my Rane," asked the boy, "may we not cut our way out through that lowland fen to the open sea and liberty?"

"'T is Odin's own device," cried the delighted helmsman, catching at his young chief's great plan. "Ho, war-wolves all, bite ye your way through the Swedish fens! Up with the serpent banner, and farewell to Olaf the Swede!"

It seemed a narrow chance, but it was the only one. Fortune favored the boy viking. Heavy rains had flooded the lands that slope down to the Maelar Lake; in the dead of night the Swedish captives and stout Norse oarsmen were set to work, and before daybreak an open cut had been made in the lowlands beneath Agnefit, or the "Rock of King Agne," where, by the town of Södertelje, the vikings' canal is still shown to travellers; the waters of the lake came rushing through the cut, and an open sea-strait waited young Olaf's fleet.

"Unship the rudder; hoist the sail aloft!" commanded Rane the helmsman "Sound war-horns all! Skoal to the Viking; skoal to the wise young Olaf!"

A strong breeze blew astern; the Norse rowers steered the

rudderless ships with their long oars, and with a mighty rush, through the new canal and over all the shallows, out into the great Norrström, or North Stream, as the Baltic Sea was called, the fleet passed in safety while the loud war-horns blew the notes of triumph.

So the boy viking escaped from the trap of his Swedish foes, and, standing by the "grim gaping dragon's head" that crested the prow of his war-ship, he bade the helmsman steer for Gotland Isle, while Sigvat the saga-man sang with the ring of triumph:

"Down the fiord sweep wind and rain;
Our sails and tackle sway and strain;
Wet to the skin
We're sound within.
Our sea-steed through the foam goes prancing,
While shields and spears and helms are glancing.
From fiord to sea,
Our ships ride free,
And down the wind with swelling sail
We scud before the gathering gale."

What a breezy, rollicking old saga it is. Can't you almost catch the spray and sea-swell in its dashing measures, boys?

Now, turn to your atlases again and look for the large island of Gotland off the south-eastern coast of Sweden, in the midst of the Baltic Sea. In the time of Olaf it was a thickly peopled and wealthy district, and the principal town, Wisby, at the northern end, was one of the busiest places in all Europe. To this attractive island the boy viking sailed with all his ships, looking for rich booty, but the Gotlanders met him with fair words and offered him so great a "scatt," or tribute, that he agreed not to molest them, and rested at the island, an unwelcome guest, through all the long winter. Early in the spring he sailed eastward to the Gulf of Riga and spread fear and terror along the coast of Finland. And the old saga tells how the Finlanders "conjured up in the night, by their witchcraft, a dreadful storm and bad weather; but the king ordered all the anchors to be weighed and sail hoisted, and beat off all night to the outside of the land. So the king's luck prevailed more than the Finlanders' witchcraft."

Then away "through the wild sea" to Denmark sailed the young pirate king, and here he met a brother viking, one Thorkell the Tall. The two chiefs struck up a sort of partnership; and coasting southward along the western shores of Denmark, they won a sea-fight in the Ringkiobing Fiord, among the "sand hills of Jutland." And so business continued brisk with this curiously matched pirate firm — a giant and a boy — until, under the cliffs of Kinlimma, in Friesland, hasty word came to the boy viking that the English king, Ethelred "The Unready," was calling for the help of all sturdy fighters to win back his heritage and crown from young King Cnut, or Canute the Dane, whose father had seized the throne of England. Quick to respond to an appeal that promised plenty of hard knocks, and the possibility of unlimited booty, Olaf, the ever ready, hoisted his blue and crimson sails and steered his war-ships over sea to help King Ethelred, the never ready. Up the Thames and straight for London town he rowed.

"Hail to the serpent banner! Hail to Olaf the Brave!" said King Ethelred, as the war-horns sounded a welcome; and on the low shores of the Isle of Dogs, just below the old city, the keels of the Norse war-ships grounded swiftly, and the boy viking and his followers leaped ashore. "Thou dost come in right good time with thy trusty dragon-ships, young King," said King Ethelred; "for the Danish robbers are full well entrenched in London town and in my father Edgar's castle."

And then he told Olaf how, "in the great trading place which is called Southwark," the Danes had raised "a great work and dug large ditches, and within had built a bulwark of stone, timber and turf, where they had stationed a large army."

"And we would fain have taken this bulwark," added the King, "and did in sooth bear down upon it with a great assault; but indeed we could make naught of it."

"And why so?" asked the young viking.

"Because," said King Ethelred, "upon the bridge betwixt the castle and Southwark have the ravaging Danes raised towers and parapets, breast high, and thence they did cast down stones and weapons upon us so that we could not prevail. And now, Sea-King, what dost thou counsel? How may we avenge ourselves of our enemies and win the town?"

Impetuous as ever, and impatient of obstacles, the young viking said: "How? why, pull thou down this bridge, King, and then may ye have free river-way to thy castle."

"Break down great London Bridge, young hero?" cried the amazed king. "How may that be? Have we a Duke Samson among us to do so great a feat?"

"Lay me thy ships alongside mine, King, close to this barricaded bridge," said the valorous boy, "and I will vow to break it down, or ye may call me caitiff and coward."

"Be it so," said Ethelred, the English king; and all the war-chiefs echoed: "Be it so!" So Olaf and his trusty Rane made ready the war-forces for the destruction of the bridge.

Old London Bridge was not what we should now call an imposing structure, but our ancestors of nine centuries back esteemed it quite a bridge. The chronicler says that it was "so broad that two wagons could pass each other upon it," and "under the bridge were piles driven into the bottom of the river."

So young Olaf and old Rane put their heads together, and decided to wreck the bridge by a bold viking stroke. And this is how it is told in the "Heimskringla," or Saga of King Olaf the Saint:

"King Olaf ordered great platforms of floating wood to be tied together with hazal bands, and for this he took down old houses; and with these, as a roof, he covered over his ships so widely that it reached over the ships' sides. Under this screen he set pillars, so high and stout that there both was room for swinging their swords, and the roofs were strong enough to withstand the stones cast down upon them."

"Now, out oars and pull for the bridge," young Olaf commanded; and the roofed-over war-ships were rowed close up to

London Bridge.

And as they came near the bridge, the chronicle says:

"There were cast upon them, by the Danes upon the bridge, so many stones and missile weapons, such as arrows and spears, that neither helmet nor shield could hold out against it; and the ships themselves were so greatly damaged that many retreated out of it."

But the boy viking and his Norsemen were there for a purpose, and were not to be driven back by stones or spears or arrows. Straight ahead they rowed, "quite up under the bridge."

"Out cables, all, and lay them around the piles," the young sea-king shouted; and the half-naked rowers, unshipping their oars, reached out under the roofs and passed the stout cables twice around the wooden supports of the bridge. The loose end was made fast at the stern of each vessel, and then, turning and heading down stream, King Olaf's twenty stout war-ships waited his word:

"Out oars!" he cried; "pull, war-birds! Pull all, as if ye were for Norway!"

Forward and backward swayed the stout Norse rowers; tighter and tighter pulled the cables; fast down upon the straining war-ships rained the Danish spears and stones; but the wooden piles under the great bridge were loosened by the steady tug of the cables, and soon with a sudden spurt the Norse war-ships darted down the river, while the slackened cables towed astern the captured piles of London Bridge. A great shout went up from the besiegers, and "now," says the chronicle, "as the armed troops stood thick upon the bridge, and there were likewise many heaps of stones and other weapons upon it, the bridge gave way; and a great part of the men upon it fell into the river, and all the others fled — some into the castle, some into Southwark." And before King Ethelred, "The Unready," could pull his ships to the attack, young Olaf's fighting-men had sprung ashore, and, storming the Southwark earthworks, carried all before them, and the battle of London Bridge was won.

And the young Olaf's saga-man sang triumphantly:

"London Bridge is broken down —
Gold is won and bright renown;
Shields resounding,
War-horns sounding,
Hildar shouting in the din!
Arrows singing,
Mail-coats ringing,
Odin makes our Olaf win!"

And perhaps, who knows, this wrecking of London Bridge so many hundred years ago by Olaf, the boy viking of fifteen, may have been the origin of the old song-game dear to so many generations of children:

"London Bridge is fallen down, fallen down, fallen down —
London Bridge is fallen down, my fair lady!"

So King Ethelred won back his kingdom, and the boy viking was honored above all others. To him was given the chief command in perilous expeditions against the Danes, and the whole defence of all the coast of England. North and south along the coast he sailed with all his war-ships, and the Danes and Englishmen long remembered the dashing but dubious ways of this young sea-rover, who swept the English coast and claimed his dues from friend and foe alike. For those were days of insecurity for merchant and trader and farmer, and no man's wealth or life was safe except as he paid ready tribute to the fierce Norse allies of King Ethelred. But soon after this, King Ethelred died, and young Olaf, thirsting for new adventures, sailed away to the south and fought his way all along the French coast as far as the mouth of the river Garonne. Many castles he captured; many rival vikings subdued; much spoil he gathered; until at last his dragon-ships lay moored under the walls of old Bordeaux, waiting for fair winds to take him around to the Straits of Gibraltar, and so on "to the land of Jerusalem."

One day, in the booty-filled "fore-hold" of his dragon-ship, the young sea-king lay asleep; and suddenly, says the old record, "he dreamt a wondrous dream."

"Olaf, great stem of kings, attend!" he heard a deep voice call; and, looking up, the dreamer seemed to see before him "a great and important man, but of a terrible appearance withal."

"If that thou art Olaf the Brave, as men do call thee," said the vision, "turn thyself to nobler deeds than vikings' ravaging and this wandering cruise. Turn back, turn back from thy purposeless journey to the land of Jerusalem, where neither honor nor fame awaits thee. Son of King Harald, return thee to thy heritage; for thou shalt be King over all Norway."

Then the vision vanished and the young rover awoke to find himself alone, save for the sleeping foot-boy across the cabin door-way. So he quickly summoned old Rane, the helmsman, and told his dream.

"'T was for thy awakening, King," said his stout old follower. "'T was the great Olaf, thine uncle, Olaf Tryggvesson the King, that didst call thee. Win Norway, King, for the portent is that thou and thine shall rule thy fatherland."

And the war-ships' prows were all turned northward again, as the boy viking, following the promise of his dream, steered homeward for Norway and a throne.

Now in Norway Earl Eric was dead. For thirteen years he had usurped the throne that should have been filled by one of the great King Olaf's line; and, at his death, his handsome young son, Earl Hakon the Fair, ruled in his father's stead. And when young King Olaf heard this news, he shouted for joy and cried to Rane:

"Now, home in haste, for Norway shall be either Hakon's heritage or mine!"

"'T is a fair match of youth 'gainst youth," said the trusty helmsman; "and if but fair luck go with thee, Norway shall be thine!"

So, from "a place called Furovald," somewhere between the mouths of Humber and of Tees, on the English coast, King Olaf, with but two stout war-ships and two hundred and twenty "well-armed and chosen persons," shook out his purple sails to the

North Sea blasts, and steered straight for Norway.

As if in league against this bold young viking the storm winds came rushing down from the mountains of Norway and the cold belt of the Arctic Circle and caught the two war-ships tossing in a raging sea. The storm burst upon them with terrific force, and the danger of shipwreck was great. "But," says the old record, "as they had a chosen company and the king's luck with them all went on well.

"Thou able chief!"

sings the faithful saga-man,

"With thy fearless crew
Thou meetest with skill and courage true
The wild sea's wrath
On thy ocean path.
Though waves mast-high were breaking round,
Thou findest the middle of Norway's ground,
With helm in hand
On Saelö's strand."

Now *Sael* was Norse for "lucky" and Saelö's Island means the lucky island.

"I'll be a lucky king for landing thus upon the Lucky Isle," said rash young Olaf, with the only attempt at a joke we find recorded of him, as, with a mighty leap, he sprang ashore where the sliding keel of his war-ship ploughed the shore of Saelö's Isle.

"True, 't is a good omen, King," said old Rane the helmsman, following close behind.

But the soil of the "lucky isle" was largely clay, moist and slippery, and as the eager young viking climbed the bank his right foot slipped, and he would have fallen had not he struck his left foot firmly in the clay and thus saved himself. But to slip at all was a bad sign in those old, half-pagan, and superstitious times, and he said, ruefully: "An omen; an omen, Rane! The king falls!"

"Nay, 't is the king's luck," says ready and wise old Rane. "Thou didst not fall, King. See; thou didst but set fast foot in this thy native soil of Norway."

"Thou art a rare diviner, Rane," laughed the young king much relieved, and then he added solemnly: "It may be so if God doth will it so."

And now news comes that Earl Hakon, with a single war-ship, is steering north from Sogne Fiord; and Olaf, pressing on, lays his two ships on either side of a narrow strait, or channel, in Sandunga Sound. Here he stripped his ships of all their war-gear, and stretched a great cable deep in the water, across the narrow strait. Then he wound the cable-ends around the capstans, ordered all his fighting-men out of sight, and waited for his rival. Soon Earl Hakon's war-ship, crowded with rowers and fighting-men, entered the strait. Seeing, as he supposed, but two harmless merchant-vessels lying on either side of the channel, the young earl bade his rowers pull between the two. Suddenly there is a stir on the quiet merchant-vessels. The capstan bars are manned; the sunken cable is drawn taut. Up goes the stern of Earl Hakon's entrapped war-ship; down plunges her prow into the waves, and the water pours into the doomed boat. A loud shout is heard; the quiet merchant-vessels swarm with mail-clad men, and the air is filled with a shower of stones, and spears, and arrows. The surprise is complete. Tighter draws the cable; over topples Earl Hakon's vessel, and he and all his men are among the billows struggling for life. "So," says the record, "King Olaf took Earl Hakon and all his men whom they could get hold of out of the water and made them prisoners; but some were killed and some were drowned."

Into the "fore-hold" of the king's ship the captive earl was led a prisoner, and there the young rivals for Norway's crown faced each other. The two lads were of nearly the same age — between sixteen and seventeen, — and young Earl Hakon was considered the handsomest youth in all Norway. His helmet was gone, his sword was lost, his ring-steel suit was sadly disarranged, and his long hair, "fine as silk," was "bound about his head with a gold ornament." Fully expecting the fate of all captives in those cruel days — instant death, — the young earl nevertheless faced his boy conqueror proudly, resolved to meet his fate like a man.

"They speak truth who say of the house of Eric that ye be handsome men," said the King, studying his prisoner's face. "But now, Earl, even though thou be fair to look upon, thy luck hath failed thee at last."

"Fortune changes," said the young earl. "We both be boys; and thou, king, art perchance the shrewder youth. Yet, had we looked for such a trick as thou hast played upon us, we had not thus been tripped upon thy sunken cables. Better luck next time."

"Next time!" echoed the king; "dost thou not know, Earl, that as thou standest there, a prisoner, there may be no 'next time' for thee?"

The young captive understood full well the meaning of the words. "Yes, King," he said; "it must be only as thou mayst determine. Man can die but once. Speak on; I am ready!" But Olaf said: "What wilt thou give me, Earl, if at this time I do let thee go, whole and unhurt?"

"'T is not what I may give, but what thou mayst take, King," the earl made answer. "I am thy prisoner; what wilt thou take to free me?"

"Nothing," said the generous young viking, advancing nearer to his handsome rival. "As thou didst say, we both be boys, and life is all before us. Earl, I give thee thy life, do thou but take oath before me to leave this my realm of Norway, to give up thy kingdom, and never to do battle against me hereafter."

The conquered earl bent his fair young head.

"Thou art a generous chief, King Olaf," he said. "I take my life as thou dost give it, and all shall be as thou wilt."

So Earl Hakon took the oath, and King Olaf righted his rival's capsized war-ship, refitted it from his own stores of booty, and thus the two lads parted; the young earl sailing off to his uncle, King Canute, in England, and the boy viking hastening eastward to Vigen, where lived his mother, the Queen Aasta, whom he had not seen for full five years.

It is harvest-time in the year 1014. Without and within the

long, low house of Sigurd Syr, at Vigen, all is excitement; for word has come that Olaf the sea-king has returned to his native land, and is even now on his way to this, his mother's house. Gay stuffs decorate the dull walls of the great-room, clean straw covers the earth-floor, and upon the long, four-cornered tables is spread a mighty feast of mead and ale and coarse but hearty food, such as the old Norse heroes drew their strength and muscle from. At the door-way stands the Queen Aasta with her maidens, while before the entrance, with thirty "well-clothed men," waits young Olaf's stepfather, wise Sigurd Syr, gorgeous in a jewelled suit, a scarlet cloak, and a glittering golden helmet. The watchers on the house-tops hear a distant shout, now another and nearer one, and soon, down the highway, they catch the gleam of steel and the waving of many banners; and now they can distinguish the stalwart forms of Olaf's chosen hundred men, their shining coats of ring-mail, their foreign helmets, and their crossleted shields flashing in the sun. In the very front rides old Rane, the helmsman, bearing the great white banner blazoned with the golden serpent, and, behind him, cased in golden armor, his long brown hair flowing over his sturdy shoulders, rides the boy viking, Olaf of Norway.

It was a brave home-coming; and as the stout young hero, leaping from his horse, knelt to receive his mother's welcoming kiss, the people shouted for joy, the banners waved, the war-horns played their loudest; and thus, after five years of wandering, the boy comes back in triumph to the home he left when but a wild and adventurous little fellow of twelve.

The hero of nine great sea-fights, and of many smaller ones, before he was seventeen, young Olaf Haraldson was a remarkable boy, even in the days when all boys aimed to be battle-tried heroes. Toughened in frame and fibre by his five years of sea-roving, he had become strong and self-reliant, a man in action though but a boy in years.

"I am come," he said to his mother and his stepfather, "to take the heritage of my forefathers. But not from Danish nor from Swedish kings will I supplicate that which is mine by right. I intend rather to seek my patrimony with battle-ax and sword, and I will so lay hand to the work that one of two things shall happen: Either I shall bring all this kingdom of Norway under my rule, or I shall fall here upon my inheritance in the land of my fathers."

These were bold words for a boy of seventeen. But they were not idle boastings. Before a year had passed, young Olaf's pluck and courage had won the day, and in harvest-time, in the year 1015, being then but little more than eighteen years old, he was crowned King of Norway in the Drontheim, or "Throne-home," of Nidaros, the royal city, now called on your atlas the city of Drontheim. For fifteen years King Olaf the Second ruled his realm of Norway. The old record says that he was "a good and very gentle man"; but history shows his goodness and gentleness to have been of a rough and savage kind. The wild and stern experiences of his viking days lived again even in his attempts to reform and benefit his land. When he who had himself been a pirate tried to put down piracy, and he who had been a wild young robber sought to force all Norway to become Christian, he did these things in so fierce and cruel a way that at last his subjects rebelled, and King Canute came over with a great army to wrest the throne from him. On the bloody field of Stiklestad, July 29, 1030, the stern king fell, says Sigvat, his saga-man,

"beneath the blows
By his own thoughtless people given."

So King Canute conquered Norway; but after his death, Olaf's son, Magnus the Good, regained his father's throne. The people, sorrowful at their rebellion against King Olaf, forgot his stern and cruel ways, and magnified all his good deeds so mightily, that he was at last declared a saint, and the shrine of Saint Olaf is still one of the glories of the old cathedral in Drontheim. And, after King Magnus died, his descendants ruled in Norway for nearly four hundred years; and thus was brought to pass the promise of the dream that, in the "fore-hold" of the great dragon-ship, under the walls of old Bordeaux, came so many years before to the daring and sturdy young Olaf of Norway, the Boy Viking.

FOOTNOTES:

[6] "Hail and Health to the Viking!"

[7] So contemptuously did those fierce old sea-kings regard a peaceful life, that they said of one who died quietly on his bed at home: "His was but a straw-death."

IV. WILLIAM OF NORMANDY: THE BOY KNIGHT.

(Afterward William the Conqueror, King of England.)
A.D. 1040.

It was a time of struggle in France. King and barons, lords and vassals, were warring against each other for the mastery. Castles were besieged, cities sacked, and fertile fields laid waste; and in that northern section of France known as the Duchy of Normandy the clash and crush of conflict raged the fiercest around the person of one brave-hearted but sorely troubled little man of twelve — William, Lord of Rouen, of the Hiesmos and of Falaise, and Duke of Normandy.

Left an orphan at eight by the death of his famous father — whom men called Robert the Magnificent before his face and Robert the Devil behind his back — the boyhood of the young duke had been full of danger and distress. And now in his gloomy castle at Rouen — which his great-grandfather, Richard the Fearless, had built nearly a hundred years before — new trouble threatened him, as word came that King Henry of France, the "suzerain," or overlord of Normandy, deeming his authority not sufficiently honored in his Norman fief, had invaded the boy's territories, and with a strong force was besieging the border castle of Tillieres, [8] scarce fifty miles to the south.

The beleaguering hosts of France swarmed round the strong-walled castle, and the herald of France demanded entrance. In the audience-hall the warden of the marches, or borders of Normandy, received him.

"Gilbert of Crispin," said the herald, "thy master and suzerain, King Henry of France, demands from thee the keys and possession of this his fortress of Tillieres, granting therefor, to thee and thy followers, pardon and safe conduct. But and if thou failest, then will he raze these walls to the ground, and give to thee and thy followers the sure and speedy death of traitors."

Bluff old Gilbert of Crispin, with scarcely restrained rage, made instant answer:

"Sir herald," he said, "tell thy master, the King of France, that Gilbert of Crispin defies and scorns him, and that he will hold this castle of Tillieres for his liege and suzerain, Duke William of Normandy, though all the carrion kites of France should flap their wings above it."

Defiance begets defiance, and both besiegers and besieged prepared for a stubborn conflict. Suddenly the watcher from the donjon spied a flurry of dust toward the north, out of the distance came hurrying forms, then the sun played on shield and lance and banneret, and the joyful shout of the watchman in the tower rang out: "Rescue! rescue and succor from our Duke!"

A band of knights rode from the French camp to intercept the new-comers. Then came a halt and parley, and just as doughty Gilbert of Crispin was preparing a sally for the support of his friends the parley ceased, the Norman knights rode straight to the castle, and a loud trumpet-peal summoned the warder to the gates. "Open; open in the name of the Duke!" came the command.

The ponderous drawbridge slowly fell, the grim portcullis rose with creak and rattle, the great gate swung open wide, and into the castle yard rode Duke William himself.

A handsome, ruddy, stalwart lad of twelve; old-looking for his years, and showing, even then, in muscle and in face, the effect of his stormy boyhood. An open, manly brow, wavy chestnut hair, and a face that told of thoughtful purpose and a strong will.

"Good Crispin," said the boy duke as his faithful liegeman came forward to greet him, "suffer me to have my will. 'T is wiser to fly your hawk at a stag-royal than a fox. Henry of France may be fair or false to us of Normandy but 't is safer in these troublous times to have him as friend rather than foe. You, in whose charge my father Duke Robert left me years ago, know well how when scarce seven years old I placed my hands between this same King Henry's and swore to be his man. I will be true to my fealty vows hap what may, and though it cometh hard to your stout Norman heart to give up without a blow what you are so loyal to defend, suffer me, as your suzerain, to give up this my fortress to my overlord. Trust me 't will be best for Normandy and for your duke."

Gilbert of Crispin grumbled and chafed at the command of his young lord, but he obeyed, and the castle which he had hoped to defend was handed over to King Henry as hostage for Normandy's faith.

And when the crafty king, who as the boy duke had wisely said was fox rather than stag-royal, was safely in possession he said, with all the stately courtesy he could assume when occasion served: "Fair Cousin William, so loyal and loving a concession as is this of thine, at a time when blows were far easier to give, merits more from me than thanks. The fealty of vassal to suzerain is well, but so fair a deed as this of thine is the height of knightly valor. And where such knightly valor doth live the knightly spurs should follow. Kneel before thy lord!"

And as the boy knelt bareheaded before him King Henry with drawn sword gave him the *accolade* — three smart taps with the flat of the sword on the shoulder and one with the palm of the hand on the cheek. Then said the king: "William of Normandy, in the name of God, St. Michael, and St. George, I dub thee knight. Be valiant, bold, and loyal. Speak the truth; maintain the right; protect the defenceless; succor the distressed; champion the ladies; vindicate thy knightly character, and prove thy knightly bravery and endurance by perilous adventures and valorous deeds. Fear God, fight for the faith, and serve thy suzerain and thy fatherland faithfully and valiantly."

So Duke William was made a knight at the earliest age at which knighthood was conferred. And he rode back to his castle at Rouen; and both there and at his neighboring castle of Vaudreuil, farther down the valley of the Seine, it was a day of pleasure and feasting for vassals and retainers when the boy knight first donned his armor and sprang to his saddle without aid of stirrup — "so tall, so manly in face, and so proud of bearing," says the old record, "that it was a sight both pleasant and terrible to see him guiding his horse's career, flashing with his sword, gleaming with his shield, and threatening with his casque and lance."

But soon, boy though he was, he had terrible work to do. Rebellion was abroad in his realm, and King Henry's foxy qualities were shown when, in spite of his promises, he still farther invaded the Norman land, and gave support to the boy's rebellious subjects. And, worse still, as if to heap additional insult on his young life, Thurstan Goz, charged with the defence of a portion of the Norman borders, rose in open rebellion and garrisoned with recreant Normans and purchased Frenchmen the castle of Falaise — not only the birthplace, but the favorite castle of the boy duke, — insolently declaring that if the lad dared attempt its release that he, Thurstan the rebel, had a plenty of raw hides with which to "tan the tanner." [9]

Frequent dangers and distresses had taught the boy to curb his sometimes fiery temper. But this special insult was past all endurance, and even his self-control was lost in indignation.

Scarce had the courserman, who had sped with the news to the duke's castle at Rouen, delivered his message than the boy flamed with rage, and turning to his guardian, Ralph of Wacey, captain-general of the armies of Normandy, he cried:

"Good cousin, this is not to be borne. I have done King Henry's will, and been faithful to my fealty vows, but this passeth even my bent. Fling out our standard. Summon every loyal Norman to our aid — knight and archer and cross-bowman. Cry *'Maslon!'* and *'Dix aie!'* [10] and let us straight against this dastard rebel at Falaise."

Quick to act whenever the need arose, the boy duke was soon leading his army of loyal Normans against the massive castle in which he first saw the light.

From one of those very turret windows which to-day still look down from this old castle on the cliffs upon the lovely valley or glen of the Ante, where Norman peasant women still wash their clothes as they did in Duke William's day, the recreant Thurstan saw the banners of the approaching host, and laughed grimly to think how he had outwitted the boy, and how those steep cliffs, or *felsens* (which give the place its name of Falaise), could never be scaled by the armor-encased troops of his young lord.

The Castle Of Falaise — Birthplace Of William The Conqueror.

But Thurstan reckoned without his host. Friendship is an even better ally than battering-rams and scaling-ladders. Duke William had played as a little child in this very town and castle of Falaise, and not a Norman peasant girl but loved and petted him, not a Norman peasant lad but was proud of the daring and muscle of the brave young duke. At one of those very washing booths in which it was said Duke Robert first saw and loved the beautiful Herleva, the tanner's daughter, a peasant girl, pounding her wash on the sloping board, saw across the treeless slopes the advancing banners of the duke. The clothes were left unpounded, and speeding to the little town, she told her news; the loyal men of Falaise flocked to meet their duke, the gates of the town were opened to him, and from the most accessible side the Norman host advanced to the assault of the massive castle walls.

Spurred on to fresh energy and immediate action by the loyalty of his townsmen and the sight of the rebel standard floating from the walls of his own castle, the boy knight led the assault upon the outworks, and proved in this, his first deed of arms, the truth of his biographer that he was one who "knew when to strike and how to strike." Catapult and balista, battering-ram and arbalast, cloth-yard shaft and javelin did their work, a breach was made in the walls, and only the darkness put a stop to the assault.

Then, spent with the conflict and fearful as to the result, Thurstan saw that rebellion against this determined boy was no child's play, and with his haughty spirit considerably humbled he sought an audience with the duke and craved pardon and easy terms of surrender.

No boy of thirteen, even in this refined and enlightened nineteenth century, can refrain from "crowing" over a defeated antagonist. It is human nature and boy-nature especially. What then must it have been in those cruel and vindictive days eight hundred years ago, when every man's hand was ready to strike, and every victor's sword was quick to destroy. But see how in even an ignoble age the manly boy can still be noble.

"Thurstan Goz," said the duke, "that you have warred against me I can forgive; that you have disgraced this the dearest estate of Duke Robert, my father, and of me his son, I can also forgive. But that you should forfeit your vows of fealty and rebelliously conspire against this your home-land of Normandy I can never forgive. I give you your life. Depart in peace. But, as you hope for life, never show yourself in this our realm again. You are banished from Normandy forever!"

The boyhood of William of Normandy seems to have been full of just such evidences as this of his love of justice, his kind-heartedness, his moral and physical courage — qualities which even in these days of universal education and grander opportunities would stamp a boy as noble and manly, and which were especially remarkable in that age of narrower views and universal ignorance, when even this just and wise boy prince could simply make a rude cross as his ducal signature.

So desirous was he for peace and quietness in his realm that, boy though he was, he stood among the foremost advocates of the measure by which the Church sought to limit crime and violence and bloodshed, by instituting what was known as the "Truce of God," and by the terms of which all men agreed to abstain from violent deeds (except in cases of actual warfare) from the night of Wednesday to the following Monday morning in each week.

All of William's biographers, however they criticise his later acts, unite in speaking of the excellences of his boyhood: of his wisdom in the choice of counsellors, and his willingness to listen to and follow their advice; of his personal goodness in an age of widespread viciousness; of his grace and skill in athletic sports and warlike exercises, and his expertness beyond all his companions in the excitements and successes of the chase.

Of this last-named pastime he was passionately fond, even from early boyhood, and few excelled him, either in the eagerness with which he followed the game, or the skill which he displayed in the hunt.

This thought came also to the two mail-clad watchers who, shielded from view by a group of large trees, looked with interest upon a youthful hunter, who, in one of the glades that broke the great stretch of forest near to beautiful Valognes, sped his cloth-yard shaft from his mighty longbow of English yew, and sent it whizzing full four hundred feet, straight to the heart of a bounding buck that dashed across the glade scarce forty yards from the ambushed watchers.

"By the mass, a wondrous hit!" exclaimed the older knight. "Why, man, he drew that shaft from nocking-point to pile. [11] I would have sworn that mortal man — let alone a lad like that — could not have drawn such a bow, or sped so true a shaft."

"There is but one lad that can do it in all Normandy, and that is yonder hunter," said the younger knight enthusiastic in spite of himself. "Hast thou not known that none but Duke William can bend Duke William's bow — a murrain on him too!"

"So, is it our quarry — is it the duke, say'st thou?" hurriedly asked the older knight. "Then the saints keep me out of range of his shaft. Draw off, he comes this way"; and grizzled Grimald de Plessis, the Saxon baron, drew still farther behind the tree-trunks as the young duke and his only companion, Golet, his merryman or fool, dashed across the glade to where the stricken stag lay dead.

But his companion, young Guy of Burgundy, fingered his light cross-bow nervously. "Ten thousand curses on this coward Truce!" he exclaimed beneath his breath as the duke, all unconscious of his danger, hurried past the ambush. "But for that I might even now speed my shaft and wing the tanner where he stoops above his game. Did'st ever see a fairer chance?"

But wary De Plessis caught the lad's uplifted arm. "Have down thy hand and bethink thee of that same Truce," he said. "'T is a wise restriction on your wayward wits, my lord count. The duke's men are much too nigh at hand to make such a bow-shot safe even for thee, and to-morrow's venture which we have in hand may be made without breaking this tyrant Truce or braving the ban of Holy Church. I would have a score of good men at my back ere I try to wing so stout a bird as he," and De Plessis and the hot-headed Guy withdrew from their dangerous ambush, while the duke, calling in his lagging followers, turned over his prize to his huntsmen and rode on to his castle.

"To-morrow's venture," of which the Saxon baron spoke, was to be the sorriest chance that had yet happened to the brave young duke. For this very Guy of Burgundy, cousin and comrade to William since his earliest days, brought up in his court, and beholden to him for many favors, and even for his knighthood, had — moved by jealousy — conspired with the foremost barons of Western Normandy to put the young duke to death. That very next night was the attempt to be made here in the duke's own castle of Valognes, away up in the north-western corner of France, some fifteen miles or so to the south of Cherbourg town — the modern naval and shipbuilding city, off which the *Kearsarge* and the *Alabama* had their famous sea-fight in the days of the American civil war — June 19, 1864.

But a well-known poet has told us that

"The best laid schemes o' mice and men
Gang aft a-gley,"

and this even the over-confident conspirators discovered. For, before they could reach the castle on the night appointed, Golet, the duke's faithful fool, had fathomed their plans, and with fleetest foot dashed into the castle and up the narrow stairway to the bedchamber of the sleeping duke.

Bang, bang, bang, came a noisy pounding on the closed door, rousing the lad, sorely tired from his day's hunting. Again and again the *pel*, or jester's staff, clamored against the door, and now the fully aroused duke caught his faithful servant's words:

"Up, up, my lord duke! Open, open! Where art thou, Duke William? Wherefore dost thou sleep? Flee, flee, or thou art a dead man! Up, up, I say! All are armed; all are marshalled; and if they capture thee, never, never wilt thou again see the light of day!"

So earnest a warning was not calculated to allow even the most tired of huntsmen to sleep. William sprang from his bed, and with nothing but a *capa*, or short, hooded cloak thrown over his half-clad body, without even clapping on his inseparable spurs, he leaped to his horse and rode for his life. All unattended he galloped through the night, fording now the shallow Doure and now the ebbing Vire, stopping for one short prayer for safety at the shrine of St. Clement, near Isigny, and speeding along the unfrequented road between Bayeux and the sea, until just before sunrise he galloped into the little hamlet of Rie or Rye, close to the shore. Foam-flecked and mud-bespattered, his flagging horse dashed past the *manoir* or castle of the lord of the hamlet whose name was Hubert.

"So, Hollo, My Lord Duke," Said Hubert, "What Taketh Thee Abroad In This Guise So Early?"

The old Norman was an early riser, and was standing at his castle gate sniffing the morning air. His ear caught the sound of hoofs, and as the lad galloped up, the stout old baron rubbed his eyes in surprise to see his sovereign in such sorry plight.

"So, hollo, my lord duke," he cried; "what taketh thee abroad in this guise so early? Is aught of danger afoot?"

"Hubert," said the duke, "dare I trust thee?"

"And why not," was the reply. "Have I ever played thee false? Speak, and speak boldly."

Then William told his story, and without a moment's hesitation the loyal baron hurried his early guest into the castle, summoned his three sons, gave the lad a fresh horse, and said to his boys: "Mount, and mount quickly. Behold your lord in dire stress. Leave him not till you have lodged him safely in Falaise."

He bade them God-speed and hurried them off none too soon, for scarce had the sounds of their horses' hoofs died away before the duke's pursuers came riding hard behind. And Hubert, apparently as good a conspirator as any of them, sent them on a wild-goose chase over the wrong road, while the boy duke, with his faithful escort of Hubert's sons, crossed the ford of Folpendant and reached Falaise at last in safety — in not a very presentable condition after his hard all-night ride for his life, but, says the old record, "what mattered that so that he was safe?"

Such a break-neck race with death [12] could have but one result. The young duke realized at last the fierceness and relentlessness of his rivals and enemies, and, sorrowing most of all at the treachery of the lad who had been his playmate and comrade in arms in mimic fight and serious quarrel, at the chase and in the tourney, he turned reluctantly for succor to the only man to whom he might rightly look for aid — his liege lord and suzerain, Henry, King of France.

That crafty and unscrupulous king, whose relations with his boy vassal had been one continual game of "fast and loose," as desire dictated or opportunity served, gave a secret chuckle of joy as Duke William and his slender escort of knights and men-at-arms rode into the palace yard at Poissy, only a few miles northwest of modern Versailles. And when at last he saw the youth an actual suppliant at his throne his thought was: "Ah ha! Duke William and Normandy are in my power at last."

But King Henry's lips seldom spoke his thoughts.

"Cousin of Normandy," he said, "you have done well and wisely to pray my aid against your rebel barons and this wicked boy of Burgundy. To whom else should you turn but to the overlord to whom your great father, Duke Robert, confided you as a sacred trust years ago?"

The lad might justly have inquired how King Henry had kept the trust his father had confided in him. But he only said:

"'T is not for me but for my father's duchy that I plead. The very life of Normandy is in jeopardy, my liege."

"And right valiantly will we relieve it, lad," the king exclaimed. "Send out your rallying-call. Summon your loyal vassals. Join force and arm with me, and the banners of France and Normandy shall wave above conquered rebels and a victorious field."

Action quickly succeeded words. An army was speedily raised. The loyal Normans of the eastern counties hurried to the standard of their young lord, and at the head of a combined French and Norman force, king and duke, in the summer of the year 1047, confronted the rebel knights under Guy of Burgundy, Grimbald de Plessis, Neel of St. Savior, and Randolf of Bayeux, on the open slopes of Val-es-dunes, or the valley of the sand-hills, not far from the town of Caen, and almost within sight of the English Channel.

Duke William led the left wing and King Henry the right. There was a shouting of battle-cries — the *Dix aie* of the loyal Normans and the *Montjoye-St. Denys* of France mingling with *St. Savior* and *St. Armand* from the rebel ranks. Then, as in a great tournament, horse and rider, shield, sword, and lance closed in desperate combat. It was a battle of the knights. King Henry went down twice beneath the thrust of Norman lances, but was on his horse again fighting valiantly in his vassal's cause, and Duke William, in this his first pitched battle, by a day of mingled courage, good fortune, prowess, and personal success, laid the basis of that wonderful career that filled his daring and victorious future, and fitted him to bear the proud though bloody title of the Conqueror. Hand to hand, not with lance but with sword, he vanquished in open conflict the champion of the rebel knights,

Hardrez of Bayeux, and ere darkness fell his enemies were vanquished and in desperate flight for life, and his power as Duke of Normandy was established finally and forever.

Great in his victory the boy knight was greater still in his generous treatment of the conquered rebels. Only one, Grimbald de Plessis, who had been the prime mover in the treason, suffered imprisonment and death. All were pardoned, and young Guy of Burgundy, like the coward he seems to have been, slipped sullenly away rather than face his generous rival and old-time playfellow, and in his distant court of Burgundy spent his after years in unsuccessful plots against his always successful rival.

And here our story of the boy William ends. Conqueror at Val-es-dunes, when yet scarcely nineteen, his course from that time on through his busy manhood, was one of unvarying success in battle and in statecraft. The wonderful victory at Senlac, or Hastings, which, on the 14th of October, 1066, gave him the throne of England, and made him both king and conqueror, has placed his name in the foremost rank of the military heroes of the world. From this point his story is known to all. It is a part of the history of our race. It is, indeed, as Palgrave the historian says:

"Magnificent was William's destiny. Can we avoid accepting him as the Founder of the predominating empire now existing in the civilized world? Never does the sun set upon the regions where the British banner is unfurled. Nay, the Stars and Stripes of the Transatlantic Republic would never have been hoisted, nor the Ganges flow as a British stream, but for Norman William's gauntleted hand."

Eight hundred years of progress have removed us far from the savagery of Duke William's day. The nations of the world are, each year, less and less ready to fly at each other's throats like "dogs of war," whenever any thing goes wrong or their "angry passions rise." The desires of to-day are largely in the direction of universal peace and brotherhood. But still we honor valor and courage and knightly and noble deeds. And though, as we study the record of that remarkable life that so changed the history of the world eight centuries back, we can see faults and vices, shortcomings and crimes even, in the stirring life of William, Duke of Normandy and King of England, still, as we look upon his spirited statue that now stands in the market-place of Falaise, almost beneath the ruined walls of the grim old castle in which he was born, and which he stormed and carried when a boy of scarce fourteen, our thoughts go back to his stormy and turbulent boyhood. And, as we do so, we see, not the Conqueror of England, the enslaver of the Saxons, the iron-handed tyrant of the Curfew-bell and the Doomsday-book, but the manly, courageous, true-hearted, perplexed, and persecuted little fellow of the old Norman days, when, spite of trouble and turmoil, he kept his heart brave, and true, and pure, and was in all things the real boy knight — in those fresh and generous days of youth, when, as Mr. Freeman, the brilliant historian of the Norman Conquest, says: "He shone forth before all men as the very model of every princely virtue."

FOOTNOTES:

[8] Tillieres, the Tuileries or tile-kiln, was old French for clay-pit or brick-yard, and is the name also of a famous French palace.

[9] Young William's mother, Herleva of Falaise, was the daughter of Fulbert, a prosperous tanner of the town, and the boy was taunted with what was esteemed his low birth — as if, indeed, an honest tanner was not the superior of a robber baron!

[10] The old Norman battle-cries.

[11] "Nocking-point to pile" in old-time archery meant the full length of the arrow from the point where it "notched" the bowstring to the arrowhead itself.

[12] The place at which young William in his flight from Valognes forded the river Vire is still called "*la voie du Duc.*" — the Duke's Way.

V. BALDWIN OF JERUSALEM: THE BOY CRUSADER.

(Known as Baldwin III., the Fifth of the Latin Kings of Jerusalem.)
A.D. 1147.

Through a flood of sunlight, cooled by mountain breezes, breaks a straggling mass of hill and plain and deep ravine crowded with gray-walled buildings, crumbling ruins, dismantled towers, glittering minarets and crosses, stout walls and rounded domes. A palace here, a broken arch or cross-crowned chapel there; narrow and untidy streets thronged with a curious crowd drawn from every land and race — Syrian and Saxon, Norman and Nubian, knight and squire, monk and minstrel, — such was Jerusalem, "city of ruins," when, seven hundred years ago, the Red-Cross banner floated from its towered walls and the Holy City stood as the capital of the short-lived and unfortunate realm of the Crusaders — the Latin kingdom of Jerusalem.

I take it for granted that most of my young readers know something of the history of the Crusades — those wonderful religious wars, when Europe overflowed into Asia and under the banner of the Cross sought by blood and blows and daring deeds to gain possession from the Saracen conquerors — or, as they were called, the "Infidel," — of the tomb of Him whose mission was "Peace on Earth; Good-Will to Men." But how many of them know any thing of that eventful and romantic chapter in the history of Palestine, when, for eighty-eight years, from the days of Duke Godfrey, greatest of the Crusaders, to the time of Saladin, greatest of the Sultans, the Holy City was governed by Christian nobles and guarded by Christian knights, drawn from the shores of Italy, the downs of Normandy, and the forests of Anjou? It is a chapter full of interest and yet but little known, and it is at about the middle of this historic period, in the fall of the year 1147, that our sketch opens.

In the palace of the Latin kings, on the slopes of Mount Moriah, a boy of fifteen and a girl of ten were leaning against an open casement and looking out through the clear September air toward the valley of the Jordan and the purple hills of Moab.

"Give me thy gittern, Isa," said the boy, a ruddy-faced youth, with gray eyes and auburn hair; "let me play the air that Réné, the troubadour, taught me yesterday. I'll warrant thee 't will set thy feet a-flying, if I can but master the strain," and he hummed over the gay Provençal measure:

"O Magali! thy witcheries
In vain shall try me!
When thou art fish, I'll fisher be
And fish for thee!"

But, bewitching little maiden though she was, the fair young Isabelle had no thought of becoming a fish. She had now found something more absorbing than the song of the troubadour.

"Nay, my lord, rather let me try the gittern," she said. "See, now will I charm this snaily from its cell with the air that Réné taught *me*," and together the two heads bent over one of the vicious little "desert snails of Egypt," which young Isabelle of Tyre had found crawling along the casement of the palace.

"Snaily, snaily, little nun,
Come out of thy cell, come into the sun;
Show me thy horns without delay,
Or I'll tear thy convent-walls away,"

sang the girl merrily, as she touched the strings of her gittern. But his snailship continued close and mute, and the boy laughed loudly as he picked up the snail and laid it on his open palm.

"'T is in vain, Isa," he said; "this surly snail is no troubadour to come out at his lady's summons. Old Hassan says the sluggards can sleep for full four years, but trust me to waken this one. So, holo! See, Isa, there be his horns — ah! oh! the Forty Martyrs grind thy Pagan shell!" he cried, with sudden vehemence, dancing around the room in pain, "the beast hath bitten me! Out, Ishmaelite!" and he flung the snail from him in a rage, while Isabelle clung to the casement laughing heartily at her cousin's mishap.

But the snail flew across the room at an unfortunate moment, for the arras parted suddenly and a tall and stalwart man, clothed in the coarse woollen gown of a palmer, or pilgrim to Jerusalem, entered the apartment just in time to receive the snail full against his respected and venerated nose.

"The saints protect us!" exclaimed the palmer, drawing back in surprise and clapping a hand to his face. "Doth the king of Jerusalem keep a catapult in this his palace with which to greet his visitors?" Then, spying the two young people, who stood in some dismay by the open casement, the stranger strode across the room and laid a heavy hand upon the boy's shoulder, while little Isa's smothered laugh changed to an alarmed and tremulous "Oh!"

"Thou unmannerly boy," said the palmer, "how dar'st thou thus assault a pilgrim to the holy shrines?"

But the lad stood his ground stoutly. "Lay off thine hand, sir palmer," he said. "Who art thou, forsooth, that doth press thy way into the private chambers of the king?"

"Nay, that is not for thee to know," replied the palmer.

"Good faith, I have a mind to shake thee well, sir page, for this thy great impertinence."

But here little Isa, having recovered her voice, exclaimed hurriedly: "O no, — not page, good palmer. He is no page; he is — — "

"Peace, Isa," the lad broke in with that peculiar wink of the left eyelid well known to every boy who deals in mischief and mystery. "Let the gray palmer tell us who *he* may be, or, by my plume, he goeth no farther in the palace here."

The burly pilgrim looked down upon the lad, who, with arms akimbo and defiant face, barred his progress. He laughed a grim and dangerous laugh. "Thou rare young malapert!" he said. "Hath, then, the state of great King Godfrey fallen so low that chattering children keep the royal doors?" Then, seizing the boy by the ear, he whirled him aside and said: "Out of my path, sir page. Let me have instant speech with the king, thy master, ere I seek him out myself and bid him punish roundly such a saucy young jackdaw as thou."

"By what token askest thou to see the king?" the boy demanded, nursing his wounded ear.

"By this same token of the royal seal," replied the palmer, and he held out to the lad a golden signet-ring, "the which I was to show to whomsoever barred my path and crave due entrance to the king for the gray palmer, Conradin."

"So, 't is the queen-mother's signet," said the boy. "There is then no gainsaying thee. Well, good palmer Conradin, thou need'st go no farther. *I* am the King of Jerusalem."

The palmer started in surprise. "Give me no more tricks, boy," he said, sternly.

"Nay, 't is no trick, good palmer," said little Isabelle, in solemn assurance. "This is the king."

The palmer saw that the little maid spoke truly, but he seemed still full of wonder, and, grasping the young king's shoulder, he held him off at arm's length and looked him over from head to foot.

"Thou the king!" he exclaimed. "Thou that Baldwin of Jerusalem whom men do call the hero of the Jordan, the paladin of the Sepulchre, the young conqueror of Bostra? Thou — a boy!"

"It ill beseemeth me to lay claim to hero and paladin," said young King Baldwin, modestly. "But know, sir pilgrim, that I am as surely King Baldwin of Jerusalem as thou art the palmer Conradin. What warrant, then, hast thou, gray palmer though thou be, to lay such heavy hands upon the king?" And he strove to free himself from the stranger's grasp.

"Thou The King!" He Exclaimed; "Thou That Baldwin Of Jerusalem Whom Men Do Call The Hero Of The Jordan!"

But the palmer caught him round the neck with a strong embrace. "What warrant, lad?" he exclaimed heartily. "Why, the warrant of a brother, good my lord. Thousands of leagues have I travelled to seek and succor thee. Little brother of Jerusalem, here am I known only as a gray palmer at the holy shrines, but from the Rhine to Ratisbon and Rome am I hailed as Conrad, King of Germany and Holy Roman Emperor!"

It was now the boy's turn to start in much surprise. "Thou the great emperor — and in palmer's garb?" he said. "Where, then, are thy followers, valiant Conrad?"

"Six thousand worn and weary knights camp under the shadow of Acre's walls," replied the emperor, sadly, "the sole remains of that gallant train of close on ninety thousand knights who followed the banner of the Cross from distant Ratisbon. Greek traitors and Arab spears have slain the rest, and I am come, a simple pilgrim, to do deep penance at the holy shrines, and thereafter to help thee, noble boy, in thy struggles 'gainst the Saracen."

"And the King of France?" asked Baldwin.

"King Louis is even now at Antioch, with barely seven thousand of his seventy thousand Frankish knights," the emperor replied. "The rest fell, even as did mine, by Greek craft, by shipwreck, and by Infidel device."

It is a sad story — the record of the Second Crusade. From first to last it tells but of disaster and distress amidst which only one figure stands out bright and brave and valorous — the figure of the youthful king, the boy Crusader, Baldwin, of Jerusalem. It was a critical time in the Crusader's kingdom. The old enthusiasm that had burned in Duke Godfrey's followers had been dulled by forty years of Syrian listlessness. Fierce foes without and treacherous feuds within harassed and weakened the Christian kingdom. Edessa, its strongest outpost, fell before the Saracens. Jerusalem was threatened. The Holy Sepulchre was in danger; and though King Baldwin was a valiant lad the old Bible saying was fast being proved: "Every kingdom divided against itself is brought to desolation." France and Germany, roused at last to action by the glowing eloquence of St. Bernard, poured their thousands eastward, and Europe felt again the tramp of armies marching under the Red-Cross banner on a new Crusade. But from Hungary to Syria disaster followed disaster, and of the thousands of knights and spearmen who entered the Crusade only a miserable remnant reached Palestine, led on by Conrad, Emperor of Germany, and Louis, King of France. The land they came to succor was full of jealousy and feud, and the brave boy king alone gave them joyful welcome. But young Baldwin had pluck and vigor enough to counterbalance a host of laggards.

"Knights and barons of Jerusalem," he said, as he and the pilgrim emperor entered the audience-hall, "'t is for us to act. Lay we aside all paltry jealousy and bickering. Our brothers from the West are here to aid us. 'T is for us to wield the sword of Godfrey and raise the banner of the Cross, and marching in the van deal death to the pagan Saracen. Up, guardians of the Holy Sepulchre, strike for the Kingdom and the Cross!"

The Syrian climate breeds laziness, but it also calls out quick passion and the fire of excitement. Catching the inspiration of the boy's earnest spirit, the whole assemblage of knights and barons, prelates and people, shouted their approval, and the audience-chamber rang again and again with the war-cry of the Crusaders, *"Dieu li volt! Dieu li volt!"* [13]

Erelong, within the walls of Acre, the three crusading kings, the monarchs of Germany, of France, and of Jerusalem, resolved to strike a sudden and terrible blow at Saracen supremacy, and to win glory by an entirely new conquest, full of danger and honor — the storming of the city of Damascus. Oldest and fairest of Syrian cities, Damascus, called by the old Roman emperors the "eye of all the East," rises from the midst of orchards and gardens, flowering vines, green meadows, and waving palms; the mountains of Lebanon look down upon it from the west, and far to the east stretches the dry and sandy plain of the great Syrian desert. Full of wealth and plenty, deemed a paradise by Saracens and Christians alike, the beautiful city offered to the eager crusading host a rich and wonderful booty.

With banners streaming and trumpets playing their loudest, with armor and lance-tips gleaming in the sun, the army of the Crusaders, a hundred thousand strong, wound down the slopes and passes of the Lebanon hills and pitched their camp around the town of Dareya, in the green plain of Damascus, scarce four miles distant from the city gates. Then the princes and leaders assembled for counsel as to the plan and manner of assault upon the triple walls.

The camp of King Baldwin and the soldiers of Jerusalem lay in advance of the allies of France and Germany, and nearer the beleaguered city, as the place of honor for the brave young leader who led the van of battle. From the looped-up entrance to a showy pavilion in the centre of King Baldwin's camp, the fair young maiden, Isabelle of Tyre, who, as was the custom of the day, had come with other high-born ladies to the place of siege, looked out upon the verdant and attractive gardens that stretched before her close up to the walls of Damascus. A lovelier scene could scarcely be imagined, and to the Crusaders, wearied with their march, under a burning July sun, across the rugged and tedious steeps of Lebanon, the rich landscape, bright with golden apricots, brilliant pomegranate blossoms, full-leaved foliage and flowering vines, all springing from a carpet of living green, was wonderfully attractive. To the little Lady Isabelle the temptation was too strong to be resisted, and she readily yielded to a suggestion from young Renaud de Chatillon, a heedless and headstrong Frankish page, who "double-dared" her, even as boys and girls do nowadays, to go flower-picking in the enemy's gardens. Together they left the pavilion, and, passing the tired outposts unperceived, strolled idly down to the green banks of the little river that flowed through the gardens and washed the walls of Damascus. The verdant river-bank was strewn thick with flowers and the fallen scarlet blossoms of the pomegranate, while luscious apricots hung within easy reach, and the deep shade of the walnut trees gave cool and delightful shelter. What wonder that the heedless young people lost all thought of danger in the beauty around them, and, wandering on a little and still a little farther from the protection of their own camp, were soon deep in the mazes of the dangerous gardens.

But suddenly they heard a great stir in the grove beyond them; they started in terror as a clash of barbaric music, of cymbals and of atabals, sounded on their ears, and, in an instant, they found themselves surrounded by a swarm of swarthy Saracens.

The Lady Isabelle was soon a struggling prisoner, but nimble young Renaud, swifter-footed and more wary than his companion, escaped from the grasp of his white-robed captor, tripped up the heels of a fierce-eyed Saracen with a sudden twist learned in the tilt-yard, and sped like the wind toward King Baldwin's camp, shouting as he ran: "Rescue, rescue from the Infidels!" Out of the Crusader's camp poured swift and speedy succor: a flight of spears and arrows came from either band, but the dividing distance was too great, and with a yell of triumph the Saracens and their fair young captive were lost in the thick shadows. Straight into King Baldwin's camp sped Renaud, still shouting: "Rescue, rescue! the Lady Isabelle is prisoner!" Straight through the aroused and swarming camp to where, within the walls of Dareya, the crusading chiefs still sat in council. Down at King Baldwin's feet he dropped, and cried breathlessly: "My lord King, the Lady Isabelle is prisoner to the Saracens!"

"Isa a prisoner!" exclaimed the young king, springing to his feet. "Rescue, rescue, my lords, for the sweet little lady of Tyre! Let who will, follow me straight to the camp of the Unbelievers!"

There was a hasty mounting of steeds among the Crusader's tents; a hasty bracing-up of armor and settling of casques; shields were lifted high and spears were laid in rest, and, followed by a hundred knights, the boy Crusader dashed impetuously from his camp and charged into the thick gardens that held his captive cousin. His action was quicker than Isabelle's captors had anticipated; for, halting ere they rode within the city, the Saracens had placed her within one of the little palisaded towers scattered through the gardens for the purpose of defence. Quick-witted and ready-eared, the little lady ceased her sobs as she heard through the trees the well-known "*Beausant!*" the war-cry of the Knights of the Temple, and the ringing shout of "A Baldwin to the rescue!" Leaning far out of the little tower, she shook her crimson scarf, and cried shrilly: "Rescue, rescue for a Christian maiden!" King Baldwin saw the waving scarf and heard his cousin's cry. Straight through the hedgeway he charged, a dozen knights at his heels; a storm of Saracen arrows rattled against shield and hauberk, but the palisades were soon forced, the swarthy captors fell before the levelled lances of the rescuers, the lady Isabelle sprang from the grasp of a Saracen rider to the arms of the king, and then, wheeling around, the gallant band sped back toward the camp ere the bewildered Saracens could recover from their surprise. But the reaction comes full soon, and now from every quarter flutter the white *bournous*, the striped *aba*, the red and yellow *keffiah* of the Saracen horsemen. They swarm from garden, and tower, and roadway, and through the opened city gates fresh troops of horsemen dash down the wide causeway that crosses the narrow river. With equal speed the camp of the Crusaders, fully roused, is pouring forth its thousands, and King Baldwin sees, with the joy of a practised warrior, that the foolish freak of a thoughtless little maiden has brought about a great and glorious battle. The rescued Isabelle is quickly given in charge of a trusty squire, who bears her back to camp, and then, at the head of the forward battle, the boy Crusader bears down upon the Saracen host, shouting: "Ho, knights and barons, gallant brothers of the Cross, follow me, and death to the Infidel."

The battle is fairly joined. The great Red-Cross banner flames out upon the breeze; behind it stream the black war-flag of the Temple and the eight-pointed Cross of the Hospital; right and left press the Oriflamme of France and the Imperial Eagle of Germany, while above the tossing mass of spears and pennons and mail-clad knights rise the mingling war-cries of "*Beausant!*" "St. Denys!" and "St. George!" and the deeper and more universal shout of the Crusaders' battle-cries: "*Christus vincit!*" and "*Dieu li volt!*" [14]

Rank on rank, with spears in rest and visors closed, the crusading knights charge to the assault. Fast behind the knights press the footmen — De Mowbray's English archers, King Louis' cross-bowmen, Conrad's spearmen, and the javelin-men of Jerusalem. Before the fury of the onset the mass of muffled Arabs and armored Saracens break and yield, but from hedge and tower and loop-holed wall fresh flights of arrows and of javelins rain down upon the Christian host, and the green gardens of Damascus are torn and trampled with the fury of the battle. Above King Baldwin's head still streams the sacred banner; his cross-handled sword is dyed with Saracen blood, and his clear young voice rings loud above the din: "Christian warriors; generous defenders of the Cross; fight — fight on as fought our fathers!"

"*Beausant!*" rings the cry of the Templars; "A Baldwin — a Baldwin for Jerusalem!" shout the boy king's knights. The "*Allah il Allah!*" and the wild war-shouts of the Saracens grow less and less defiant; the entrenchments are stormed, the palisades and towers are forced, the enemy turn and flee, and by the "never-failing valiancy" of the boy Crusader and his followers the gardens of Damascus are in the hands of the Christian knights.

But now fresh aid pours through the city gates. New bodies of Saracens press to the attack, and, led in person by Anar, Prince of Damascus, the defeated host rallies for a final stand upon the verdant river-banks of the clear-flowing Barada.

Again the battle rages furiously. Still Baldwin leads the van, and around his swaying standard rally the knights of Jerusalem and the soldier-monks of the Temple and the Hospital. Twice are they driven backward by the fury of the Saracen resistance, and young Renaud de Chatillon, battling bravely to retrieve his thoughtless action, which brought on the battle, is forced to yield to another lad of eleven, a brown-faced Kurdish boy, who in after years is to be hailed as the conqueror of the Crusaders — — Saladin, the greatest of the Sultans. The battle wavers. The French knights can only hold their ground in stubborn conflict; the heathen mass grows denser round the Red-Cross banner, the soldiers of Jerusalem are thrown into disorder, and the boy-leader's horse, pierced by a spear-thrust, falls with his rider on a losing field. "*Allah il Allah!*" rings the shrill war-cry of the Turkish host, and the Crescent presses down the Cross. But hark! a new cry swells upon the air. "A Conrad! Ho, a Conrad! Rescue for the Cross!" and through the tangled and disordered mass of the cavalry of France and Palestine bursts the stalwart German emperor and a thousand dismounted knights. The Saracen lines fall back before the charge, while in bold defiance the sword of the emperor gleams above his crest. As if in acceptance of his unproclaimed challenge, a gigantic Saracen emir, sheathed in complete armor, strides out before the pagan host, and the fiercely raging battle stops on the instant, while the two great combatants face each other alone. Their great swords gleam in the air. With feint and thrust, and stroke and skilful parry the champions wage the duel of the giants, till suddenly, in one of those feats of strength and skill that stand out as a marvellous battle-act, the sword of the emperor with a single mighty stroke cleaves through the Saracen's armor-covered body, and the gigantic emir, cut completely in twain, falls bleeding at his conqueror's feet. The Turks break in dismay as their champion falls. Young Baldwin rallies his disordered forces, the war-cries mingle with the trumpet-peal, and, on foot, at the head of their knights, the two kings lead one last charge against the enemy and drive the fleeing host within the city walls. With shouts of victory, the Christian army encamp upon the field their valor has conquered, and Damascus is almost won.

Within the city, now filled with fears of plunder and of death, preparations for flight were made, and in the great mosque women and children invoked the aid of Mahomet to shield them from an enemy more relentless than Arab or Saracen — a host whose banner-cry was dark and terrible: "Cursed be he who does not stain his sword with blood." The city seemed doomed to capture. But — "there is many a slip 'twixt the cup and the lip." In the camp of the Crusaders the exultant leaders were already quarrelling over whose domain the conquered city should be when once its gates were opened to Christian victors. The Syrian princes, the great lords of the West, the monkish Knights of the Temple and of the Hospital, alike claimed the prize, and the old fable of the hunters who fought for the possession of the lion's skin even before the lion was captured was once more illustrated. For, meantime, in the palace at Damascus, the captive page Renaud stood before the Saracen Prince Anar, and the Prince asked the boy: "As between thine honor and thy head, young Christian, which wouldst thou desire to keep?"

"So please your Highness," replied the wise and politic young page, "my honor, if it may be kept with my head; but if not — why then, what were mine honor worth to me without my head?"

"Thou art a shrewd young Frank," said the Prince Anar. "But thou mayst keep thy head and, perchance, thine honor too, if that thou canst hold thy ready tongue in check. Bear thou this scroll in secret to the Nazarene whom men do call Bernard, Grand Master of those dogs of Eblis, the Knights of the Temple, and, hark ye, see that no word of this scroll cometh to the young King Baldwin, else shall the bow-strings of my slaves o'ertake thee. Go; thou art free!"

"My life upon the safe delivery of thy scroll, great Prince," said young Renaud, overjoyed to be freed so easily, and, soon in the Crusaders' camp, he sought the Grand Master and handed him the scroll in secret. The face of the Templar was dark with envy and anger, for his counsels and the claims of the Syrian lords had been set aside, and the princedom of Damascus which he had coveted had been promised to a Western baron.

"So," said the Grand Master, as he read the scroll, "the Count of Flanders may yet be balked. What says the emir? Three casks of bezants and the city of Cæsarea for the Templars if this siege be raised. 'T is a princely offer and more than can be gained from these Flemish boors."

"Gallant lords and mighty princes," he said, with well-assumed candor, returning to the council. "'T is useless for us to hope to force the gates through this mass of gardens, where men do but fight in the dark. Rather let us depart to the desert side of the city, where, so say my spies, the walls are weaker and less stoutly protected. These may soon be carried. Then may we gain the city for the noble Count of Flanders, ere that the Emir Noureddin, who, I learn, is coming with a mighty force of Infidels, shall succor the city and keep it from the soldiers of the Cross."

This craftily given advice seemed wise, and the crusading camp was quickly withdrawn from the beautiful and well-watered gardens to the dry and arid desert before the easterly walls of the city. Fatal mistake! the walls proved stout and unassailable, the desert could not support the life of so large an army, whose supplies were speedily wasted, and through the gardens the Christians had deserted fresh hosts of Arabs poured into the city. Victory gave place to defeat and rejoicing to despair. Days of fruitless assault were followed by nights of dissension, and finally the crusading host, worn by want and divided in counsel, abruptly ended a siege they could no longer maintain. But in the final council young Baldwin pleaded for renewed endeavor.

"And is it thus, my lords," he said, "that ye do give up the fairest prize in Syria, and stand recreant to your vows as valiant soldiers of the Cross?"

Conrad the Emperor quitting the Crusade.

"King Baldwin," said Conrad, "thou art a brave and gallant youth, and were all like thee, our swords had not been drawn in vain. But youth and valor may not hope to cope with greed. We are deceived. We have suffered from treason where it should have least been feared, and more deadly than Saracen arrows are the secret stabs of thy barons of Syria."

"Now, by the Forty Martyrs," cried the young king hotly, "what thou dost claim I may not disprove by words; for here have been strange and secret doings. But for the honor of my country and my crown I may not idly listen to thy condemning speech. I dare thee to the battle-test, emperor and champion though thou be. Conrad of Germany, there lies my gage!"

"Brave youth," said Conrad, picking up the boy's mailed glove, so impetuously flung before him, and handing it to Baldwin with gentle courtesy, "this may not be. For even did not our vows under the 'Truce of God' forbid all personal quarrels, it is not for such a noble-hearted lad as thou to longer stand the champion for traitors."

So the victory, almost assured by the intrepidity of the boy Crusader, was lost through the treachery of his followers; but it is at least some satisfaction to know that the betrayers were themselves betrayed, and that the three casks of golden bezants proved to be when opened but worthless brass.

King Louis and Conrad the Emperor returned to their European dominions in anger and disgust.

The Second Crusade, which had cost so terribly in life and treasure, was a miserable failure, with only a boy's bravery to light up its dreary history. Sadly disappointed at the result of his efforts, young Baldwin still held his energy and valor unsubdued. For years he maintained his kingdom intact in the midst of intrigue and corruption, and, victorious over the Saracens at the battle of the Mount of Olives and at the Siege of Ascalon, he proved his right to be entitled a successful leader and "the model knight."

Free-handed, chivalrous, handsome, brave, and generous, he is a pleasant picture to contemplate amidst the darkness, distrust, and greed of those old crusading days. Beloved by all alike — Saracen as well as Christian — his name has come down to us as that of "the most high-minded of the Latin kings of Jerusalem."

Poisoned by his Arab physician, who loved the young king while hating so stout a foe to the cause of Mahomet, he died at thirty-three, mourned by all Jerusalem; even his generous foe, the Saracen Noureddin, refusing to take advantage of his rival's death. "Allah forbid," said this chivalrous Oriental, "that I should disturb the proper grief of a people who are weeping for the loss of so good a king, or fix upon such an opportunity to attack a kingdom which I have now no reason to fear."

The history of the Crusades is the story of two hundred years of strife and battle, relieved only by some bright spots when the flash of a heroic life lights up the blackness of superstition and of cruelty. And among its valiant knights, equal in honor and courage and courtesy with Godfrey and Tancred and Richard of England and Saladin and St. Louis, will ever stand the name and fame of this gallant young ruler of the short-lived Latin kingdom of Jerusalem — Baldwin, the Boy Crusader.

FOOTNOTES:

[13] "It is the will of God!"

[14] "Christ conquers," and "It is the will of God."

VI. FREDERICK OF HOHENSTAUFEN: THE BOY EMPEROR.

(Afterward Frederick the Second, Emperor of Germany.)
A.D. 1207.

Gleaming with light and beauty, from the wavy sea-line where the blue Mediterranean rippled against the grim fortress of Castellamare to the dark background of olive groves and rising mountain walls, Palermo, "city of the golden shell," lay bathed in all the glory of an Italian afternoon one bright spring day in the year 1207.

Up the Cassaro, or street of the palace, and out through the massive gate-way of that curious old Sicilian city, — half Saracen, half Norman in its looks and life, — a small company of horsemen rode rapidly westward to where the square yellow towers of La Zisa rose above its orange groves. Now La Zisa was one of the royal pleasure-houses, a relic of the days when the swarthy Saracens were lords of Sicily.

In the sun-lit gardens of La Zisa, a small but manly-looking lad of thirteen, with curly, golden hair and clear blue eyes, stood beneath the citron trees that bordered a beautiful little lake. A hooded falcon perched upon his wrist, and by his side stood his brown-skinned attendant, Abderachman the Saracen.

"But will it stay hooded, say'st thou?" the boy inquired, as he listened with satisfaction to the tinkling bells of the nodding bird which Abderachman had just taught him to hood. "Can he not shake it off?"

"Never fear for that, little Mightiness," the Saracen replied. "He is as safely blinded as was ever the eagle of Kairewan, whose eyes the Emir took for his crescent-tips, or even as thou art, O *el Aaziz*, [15] by thy barons of Apulia." [16]

The look of pleasure faded from the boy's face.

"Thou say'st truly, O Abderachman," he said. "What am I but a hooded falcon? I, a king who am no king! Would that thou and I could fly far from this striving world, and in those great forests over sea of which thou hast told me, could chase the lion like bold, free hunters of the Berber hills."

"Wait in patience, O *el Aaziz*; to each man comes his day," said the philosophic Saracen. "What says the blessed Koran: 'Allah is all-sufficient and propitious to such as put their trust in him.'"

But now there was heard a rustle of the citron hedge, a clatter of hoofs rang on the shell-paved roadway, and the armed band that we saw spurring through Palermo's gates drew rein at the lake-side. The leader, a burly German knight, who bore upon his crest a great boar's head with jewelled eyes and gleaming silver tusks, leaped from his horse and strode up to the boy. His bow of obeisance was scarcely more than a nod.

"Your Highness must come with me," he said, "and that at once."

The boy looked at him in protest. "Nay, Baron Kapparon, — am I never to be at my ease?" he asked. "Let me, I pray thee, play out my day here at La Zisa, even as thou didst promise me."

"Tush, boy; promise must yield to need," said the Knight of the Crested Boar. "The galleys of Diephold of Acerra even now ride in the Cala port, and think'st thou I will yield thee to his guidance? Come! At the palace wait decrees and grants which thou must sign for me ere the Aloe-stalk shall say us nay."

"Must!" cried the boy, as an angry flush covered his face; "who sayeth '*must*' to the son of Henry the Emperor? Who sayeth 'must' to the grandson of Barbarossa? Stand off, churl of Kapparon! To me, Sicilians all! To me, sons of the Prophet!" and, breaking away from the grasp of the burly knight, young Frederick of Hohenstaufen dashed across the small stone bridge that led to the marble pavilion in the little lake. But only Abderachman the Saracen crossed to him. The wrath of the Knight of Kapparon was more dreaded than the commands of a little captive king.

The burly baron laughed a mocking laugh. "Well blown, *ser Sirocco*!" [17] he said, insolently, "but for all that, your Mightiness, I fear me, must bide with me, churl though I be. Come, we waste words!" and he moved toward the lad, who stood at bay upon the little bridge.

Young Frederick slipped his falcon's leash. "Cross at thy peril, Baron Kapparon!" he cried; "one step more, and I unhood my falcon and send him straight to thy disloyal eyes. Ware the bird! His flight is certain, and his pounce is sharp!" The boy's fair face grew more defiant as he spoke, and William of Kapparon, who knew the young lad's skill at falconry, hesitated at the threat.

But as boy and baron faced each other in defiance, there was another stir of the citron hedge, and another rush of hurrying hoofs. A second armed band closed in upon the scene, and a second knightly leader sprang to the ground. A snow-white plume trailed over the new-comer's crest, and on his three-cornered shield was blazoned a solitary aloe-stalk, sturdy, tough, and unyielding.

"Who threatens the King of Sicily?" he demanded, as, sword in hand, he stepped upon the little bridge.

The German baron faced his new antagonist. "So! is it thou, Count Diephold; is it thou, Aloe of Acerra?" he said. "By what right dar'st thou to question the Baron of Kapparon, guardian of the king, and Chief Captain of Sicily?"

"'Guardian,' forsooth! 'Chief Captain,' say'st thou?" cried the Count of Acerra, angrily. "Pig of Kapparon, robber and pirate, yield up the boy! I, who was comrade of Henry the Emperor, will stand guardian for his son. Ho, buds of the Aloe, strike for your master's weal!"

There is a flash of steel as the two leaders cross ready swords. There is a rush of thronging feet as the followers of each prepare for fight. There is a mingling of battle-cries — "Ho, for the Crested Boar of Kapparon!" "Stand, for the Aloe of Acerra!" — when for the third time the purple citron-flowers sway and break, as a third band of armed men spur to the lake-side. Through the green of the foliage flashes the banner of Sicily, — the golden eagle on the blood-red field, — and the ringing voice of a third leader rises above the din. "Ho, liegemen of the Church! rescue for the ward of the Pope! Rescue for the King of Sicily!"

The new-comer, Walter of Palear, the "fighting Bishop of Catania" (as he was called) and Chancellor of Sicily, reined in his horse between the opposing bands of the Boar and the Aloe. His richly broidered cope, streaming back, showed his coat of mail beneath, as, with lifted sword, he shouted:

"Hold your hands, lords of Apulia! stay spears and stand aside. Yield up the king to me — to me, the Chancellor of the realm!"

"Cross At Thy Peril, Baron Kapparon," Cried Frederick Of Hohenstaufen.

"Off now, thou false Chancellor!" cried Count Diephold. "Think'st thou that the revenues of Sicily are for thy treasure-chest alone? Ho, Boars and Aloes both; down with this French fox, and up with Sicily!"

"Seize the boy and hold him hostage!" shouted William of Kapparon, and with extended arm he strode toward poor little Frederick. With a sudden and nimble turn, the boy dodged the clutch of the baron's mailed fist, and putting one hand on the coping of the bridge, without a moment's hesitation, he vaulted over into the lake. Abderachman the Saracen sprang after him.

"How now, thou pig-headed pirate of Kapparon," broke out Count Diephold; "thou shalt pay dearly for this, if the lad doth drown!"

But Frederick was a good swimmer, and the lake was not deep. The falcon on his wrist fluttered and tugged at its jess, disturbed by this unexpected bath; but the boy held his hand high above his head and, supported by the Saracen, soon reached the shore. Here the retainers of the Chancellor crowded around him, and springing to the saddle of a ready war-horse, the lad shouted: "Ho, for Palermo, all! which chief shall first reach St. Agatha's gate with me, to him will I yield myself!" and, wheeling his horse, he dashed through the mingled bands and sped like an arrow through the gardens of La Zisa.

The three contesting captains looked at one another in surprise.

"The quarry hath slipped," laughed Count Diephold. "By St. Nicholas of Myra, though, the lad is of the true Suabian eagle's brood. Try we the test, my lords."

There was a sudden mounting of steeds, a hurrying gallop after the flying king; but the Chancellor's band, being already in the saddle, had the advantage, and as young King Frederick and Walter the Chancellor passed under St. Agatha's pointed arch, the knights of the Crested Boar and of the Aloe-stalk saw in much disgust the great-gate close in their faces, and they were left on the wrong side of Palermo's walls, — outwitted by a boy.

But the baffled knights were not the men to give up the chase so easily. Twenty Pisan galleys, manned by Count Diephold's fighting men, lay in the Cala port of Palermo. That very night, they stormed under the walls of Castellamare, routed the Saracens of the royal guard, sent Walter the Chancellor flying for his life toward Messina; and, with young Frederick in his power, Diephold, the usurping Count of Acerra, ruled Sicily in the name of the poor little king.

In the royal palace at Palermo, grand and gorgeous with columns and mosaics and gilded walls, this boy of thirteen — Frederick of Hohenstaufen, Emperor-elect of Germany, King of Sicily, and "Lord of the World" — sat, the day after his capture by Count Diephold, sad, solitary, and forlorn.

The son of Henry the Sixth of Germany, the most victorious but most cruel of the Hohenstaufen emperors, and of Constance the Empress, daughter of Roger, the great Norman King of Sicily, Frederick had begun life on December the twenty-sixth, 1194, as heir to two powerful kingdoms. His birth had been the occasion of great rejoicings, and vassal princes and courtier poets had hailed him as "the Imperial Babe, the Glory of Italy, the Heir of the Cæsars, the Reformer of the World and the Empire!" When but two years old he had been proclaimed King of the Romans and Emperor-elect of Germany, and, when but three, he had, on the death of his father, been crowned King of Sicily and Apulia, in the great cathedral of Palermo.

But in all those two sovereignties, no sadder-hearted nor lonelier lad could have been found than this boy of thirteen, this solitary and friendless orphan, this Frederick of Hohenstaufen, the boy emperor. In Germany his uncle, Philip of Suabia, disputed with Otho of Brunswick for the imperial crown. And beautiful Sicily, the land of his birth, the land over which he was acknowledged as king, was filled with war and blood. From the lemon groves of Messina to the flowery slopes of Palermo, noble and priest, Christian and Saracen, French and German, strove for power and ravaged the land with fire and sword. Deprived sometimes of even the necessities of life, deserted by those who should have stood loyal to him, often hungry and always friendless, shielded from absolute want only by the pity of the good burghers of Palermo, used in turn by every faction and made the excuse for every feud, this heir to so great power was himself the most powerless of kings, the most unhappy of boys. And now, as he sits in his gleaming palace, uncertain where to turn for help, all his sad young heart goes into an appealing letter which has come down to us across the centuries, and a portion of which is here given to complete the dismal picture of this worried young monarch of long ago:

"To all the kings of the world and to all the princes of the universe, the innocent boy, King of Sicily, called Frederick: Greeting in God's name! Assemble yourselves, ye nations; draw nigh, ye princes, and see if any sorrow be like unto my sorrow! My parents died ere I could know their caresses, and I, a gentle lamb among wolves, fell into slavish dependence upon men of various tribes and tongues. My daily bread, my drink, my freedom, all are measured out to me in scanty proportion. No king am I. I am ruled, instead of ruling. I beg favors, instead of granting them. Again and again I beseech you, O ye princes of the earth, to aid me to withstand slaves, to set free the son of Cæsar, to raise up the crown of the kingdom, and to gather together again the scattered people!"

But it is a long lane that has no turning, and before many months another change came in the kaleidoscope of this young king's fortunes. Pope Innocent the Third had been named by the Empress Constance as guardian of her orphaned boy. To him Walter the Chancellor appealed for aid. Knights and galleys were soon in readiness. Palermo was stormed. Count Diephold was overthrown and imprisoned in the castle dungeon. Kapparon and his Pisan allies and Saracen serfs were driven out of Sicily, and the "Son of Cæsar" reigned as king once more. Then came a new alliance. Helped on by the Pope, a Spanish friendship ripened into a speedy marriage. Frederick was declared of age when he reached his fourteenth birthday, and a few months after, on the fifteenth of August, 1209, amid great rejoicings which filled Palermo with brilliancy and crowded its narrow and crooked streets with a glittering throng, the "Boy of Apulia," as he was called, was married to the wise and beautiful Constance, the daughter of Alfonso, King of Arragon. This alliance gave the young husband the desired opportunity; for, with five hundred foreign knights at his back he asserted his authority over his rebellious subjects as King of Sicily. The poor little prince, whose childhood had known only misfortune and unhappiness, became a prince indeed, and, boy though he was, took so manly and determined a stand that, ere the year was out, his authority was supreme from the walls of Palermo to the Straits of Messina.

Meantime, in Germany, affairs had been going from bad to worse. Frederick's uncle, Philip of Suabia, had been assassinated at Bamberg, and Otho of Brunswick, head of the House of Guelf, crossed the Alps, was crowned Emperor at Rome in defiance of young Frederick's claim to the Imperial throne, and marched into Southern Italy, threatening the conquest of his boy rival's Sicilian kingdom.

Again trouble threatened the youthful monarch. Anxious faces looked seaward from the castle towers; and, hopeless of withstanding any attack from Otho's hardy and victorious troops, Frederick made preparations for flight when once his gigantic rival should thunder at Palermo's gates.

"Tidings, my lord King; tidings from the north!" said Walter the Chancellor, entering the king's apartment one bright November day in the year 1211. "Here rides a galley from Gaeta in the Cala port, and in it comes the Suabian knight Anselm von Justingen, with a brave and trusty following. He beareth word to thee, my lord, from Frankfort and from Rome."

"How, then; has Otho some new design against our crown?" said Frederick. "I pray thee, good Chancellor, give the Knight of Suabia instant audience."

And soon, through the Gothic door-way of that gorgeous palace of the old Norman and older Saracen lords of Sicily, came the bluff German knight Anselm von Justingen, bringing into its perfumed air some of the strength and resoluteness of his sturdy Suabian breezes. With a deep salutation, he greeted the royal boy.

"Hail, O King!" he said. "I bring thee word of note. Otho, the Guelf, whom men now call Emperor, is speeding toward the north. Never more need Sicily fear his grip. The throne which he usurps is shaken and disturbed. The world needs an emperor who can check disorders and bring it life and strength. Whose hand may do this so surely as thine — the illustrious Lord Frederick of the grand old Hohenstaufen line, the elect King of the Romans, the Lord of Sicily?"

Frederick's eye flashed and his cheek flushed at the grand prospect thus suddenly opened before him. But he replied slowly and thoughtfully.

"By laws human and by right divine," he said, "the Holy Roman Empire is my inheritance. But canst thou speak for the princes of the empire?"

"Ay, that can I," said the knight; "I bear with me papers signed and sent by them. We have each of us examined as to our will. We have gone through all the customary rights. And we all in common, O King, turn our eyes to thee."

"I thank the princes for their faith and fealty," said Frederick; "but can they be trusty liegemen to a boy emperor?"

"Though young in years, O King," said the Suabian, "thou art old in character; though not fully grown in person, thy mind hath been by nature wonderfully endowed. Thou dost exceed the common measure of thine equals; thou art blest with virtues before thy day, as doth become one of the true blood of that august stock, the Cæsars of Germany. Thou wilt surely increase the honor and might of the empire and the happiness of us, thy loyal subjects."

"And the Pope?" queried the boy; for in those days the Pope of Rome was the "spiritual lord" of the Christian world. To him all emperors, kings, and princes owed allegiance as obedient vassals. To assume authority without the Pope's consent and blessing meant trouble and excommunication. Frederick knew this, and knew also that his former guardian, Pope Innocent, had, scarce two years before, himself crowned his rival Otho of Brunswick as Emperor of Germany.

"I am even now from Rome," replied Von Justingen; "and the Holy Father, provoked beyond all patience at the unrighteous ways of this emperor, falsely so called, hath excommunicated Otho, hath absolved the princes from their oath of fealty, and now sends to thee, Frederick of Hohenstaufen, his blessing and his bidding that thou go forward and enter upon thine inheritance."

The young Sicilian sat for some moments deep in thought. It was a tempting bait — this of an imperial crown — to one who felt it to be his by right, but who had never dared to expect nor aspire to it.

"Von Justingen," he said at last, "good knight and true I know thou art, loyal to the House of Staufen, and loyal to thy German fatherland. 'T is a royal offer and a danger-fraught attempt. But what man dares, that dare I! When duty calls, foul be his fame who shrinketh from the test. The blood of kings is mine; like a king, then, will I go forward to my heritage, and win or die in its achieving!"

"There flashed the Hohenstaufen fire," said the delighted Von Justingen; "there spoke the spirit of thy grandsire, the glorious old Kaiser Red Beard! Come thou with me to Germany, my prince. We will make thee Cæsar indeed, though the false Otho and all his legions are thundering at Frankfort gates."

So, in spite of the entreaties of his queen, and the protests of his Sicilian lords, who doubted the wisdom of the undertaking, the young monarch hurried forward the preparations for his perilous attempt. The love of adventure, which has impelled many another boy to face risk and danger, flamed high in the heart of this lad of seventeen, as, with undaunted spirit, he sought to press forward for the prize of an imperial throne. On March the eighteenth, 1212, the "Emperor of the Romans Elect," as he already styled himself, set out from orange-crowned Palermo on the "quest for his heritage" in the bleak and rugged north. The galley sped swiftly over the blue Mediterranean to the distant port of Gaeta, and upon its deck the four chosen comrades that formed his little band gathered around the fair-haired young prince, who, by the daring deeds that drew him from Palermo's sun-lit walls, was to make for himself a name and fame that should send him down to future ages as *Stupor Mundi Fredericus* — "Frederick, the Wonder of the World!" In all history there is scarcely to be found a more romantic tale of wandering than this story of the adventures of young Frederick of Hohenstaufen in search of his empire.

From Palermo to strong-walled Gaeta, the "Gibraltar of Italy," from Gaeta on to Rome, he sailed with few adventures, and here he knelt before the Pope, who, as he had crowned and discrowned Otho of Brunswick, the big and burly rival of his fair young ward, now blessed and aided the "Boy from Sicily," and helped him on his way with money and advice. From Rome to Genoa, under escort of four Genoese galleys, the boy next cautiously sailed; for all the coast swarmed with the armed galleys of Pisa, the staunch supporter of the discrowned Otho. With many a tack and many a turn the galleys headed north, while the watchful look-outs scanned the horizon for hostile prows. On the first of May, the peril of Pisa was past, and Genoa's gates were opened to receive him. Genoa was called the "door" to his empire, but foes and hardships lay in wait for him behind the friendly door. On the fifteenth of July, the boy and his escort of Genoese lancers climbed the steep slopes of the Ligurian hills and struck across the plains of Piedmont for the walls of Pavia, the "city of the hundred towers." The gates of the grand old Lombard capital flew open to welcome him, and royally attended, with a great crimson canopy held above his head, and knights and nobles following in his train, the "Child of Apulia" rode through the echoing streets.

But Milan lay to the north, and Piacenza to the south, both fiercely hostile cities, while the highway between Pavia and Cremona rang with the war-cries of the partisans of Otho, the Guelf. So, secretly, and at midnight, the Pavian escort rode with the boy out through their city gates, and moved cautiously along the valley of the Po, to where, at the ford of the Lambro, the knights of Cremona waited in the dark of an early Sunday morning to receive their precious charge. And none too soon did they reach the ford; for, scarcely was the young emperor spurring on toward Cremona, when the Milanese troops, in hot pursuit, dashed down upon the returning Pavian escort, and routed it with great loss. But the boy rode on unharmed; and soon Cremona, since famous for its wonderful violins, hailed the young adventurer, so says the record, "as if he were an angel of the Lord."

From Cremona on to Mantua, and then on to Verona, the

boy was passed along by friendly hands and vigilant escorts, until straight before him the mighty wall of the Alps rose, as if to bar his further progress. But through the great hill-rifts stretched the fair valley of the Adige; and from Verona, city of palaces, to red-walled Trent, the boy and his Veronese escort hurried on along the banks of the swift-flowing river. Midway between the two cities, his escort turned back; and with but a handful of followers the young monarch demanded admittance at the gates of the old Roman town, which, overhung by great Alpine precipices, guards the southern entrance to the Tyrol. Trent received him hesitatingly; and, installed in the bishop's palace, he and his little band sought fair escort up the valley and over the Brenner pass, the highway into Germany. But now came dreary news.

"My lord King," said the wavering Bishop of Trent, undecided which side to favor, "'t is death for you to cross the Brenner. From Innspruck down to Botzen the troops of Otho of Brunswick line the mountain ways, and the Guelf himself, so say my coursermen, is speeding on to trap your Mightiness within the walls of Trent."

Here was a dilemma. But trouble, which comes to "Mightinesses," as well as to untitled boys and girls, must be boldly faced before it can be overcome.

"My Liege," said the Knight of Suabia, stout Anselm von Justingen, "before you lie the empire and renown; behind you Italy and defeat. Which shall it be?"

"The empire or death!" said the resolute boy.

"But Otho guards the Brenner pass, my lords," said the bishop.

"Is there none other road but this?" asked Frederick.

"None," replied Von Justingen, "save, indeed, the hunter's track across the western mountains to the Grisons and St. Gall. But it is beset with perils and deep with ice and snow."

"The greater the dangers faced, the greater the glory gained," said plucky young Frederick. "Now, who will follow me, come danger or come death, across the mountains yonder to the empire and to fortune?" and every man of his stout little company vowed to follow him, and to stand by their young master, the Emperor-elect.

So it was that, in the first months of the early fall, with a meagre train of forty knights, the boy emperor boldly climbed the rugged Alpine slopes, mounting higher and higher, and braving the dangers of glacier and avalanche, blind paths and storm and cold, pressed manfully on toward the peril of an uncertain empire.

But though the risk was great, no one was merrier than he. His inseparable falcon flew at many a quarry, and his hunting-horn echoed gayly from cliff to cliff. And when a mighty *urus*, almost the last of the great Alpine elks, fell beneath his spear, a shout of joy went up, as German and Italian knights hailed him as a worthy successor of the greatest of Hohenstaufen huntsmen, his grandfather Barbarossa, the old Kaiser Red Beard.

Thus, in much peril, but safely and swiftly, the Alpine heights were crossed, and down the rugged slopes the travel-worn band descended to the valley of the Plessaur and the quaint old town of Coire. Coming all unannounced into the little town, the fair face and frank ways of the boy captivated the good Bishop of Coire, whose word was law in that mountain land. Still they pushed on, and, winding along the fair valley of the Rhine, struck across the hills toward the queer old abbey-town of St. Gall; and, with only sixty knights and a few spearmen of Appenzell, the young monarch climbed the steps of the Ruppen, the last of the Alpine passes that had separated him from the land of his forefathers.

But now comes the word that Otho and his knights, hurrying around from Bregenz, are on the track of the boy, and certain of his capture. On through St. Gall and along the gleaming lake-side the young emperor hurries, and, riding down the last of the Alpine slopes, he sees in the distance the walls of the strong old city of Constance glittering in the sun.

"Ride ye forward, my lords," said the sturdy Von Justingen

to the Bishop of Coire and the Abbot of St. Gall, who rode with the king. "Gain ye due welcome for the emperor. For if the Bishop of Constance waver in his allegiance, and we may not win fair entrance into Constance town, we are lost indeed," and accompanied by the Archbishop of Bari and ten trusty knights the two mountain prelates rode on ahead.

Soon a messenger who has been sent forward comes spurring back. "Haste ye, my Liege!" he cries. "Otho is already in sight; his pennons have been seen by the look-out on the city towers."

The hurrying hoofs of the royal train clatter over the drawbridge and through the great gate. Constance is won! but, hard behind, a cloud of dust marks the swift approach of young Frederick's laggard rival, Otho, the Guelf.

His herald's trumpet sounds a summons, and the still hesitating Bishop of Constance with the Archbishop of Bari and the Abbot of St. Gall, backed by the spearmen of the city band, stand forward on the walls.

"What ho, there, warders of the gate!" came the summons of the herald; "open, open ye the gates of Constance to your master and lord, Otho the Emperor!"

The thronging spear-tips and the swaying crests of Otho's two hundred knights flashed in the sun, and the giant form of the big Brunswicker strode out before his following. The sight of his dreaded master almost awed the Bishop of Constance into submission, but the voice of young Frederick's stanch friend and comrade, Berard, Archbishop of Bari, rang out clear and quick.

"Tell thy master, Otho of Brunswick," he said, "that Constance gates open only at the bidding of their rightful lord, Frederick of Hohenstaufen, Emperor of the Romans and King of Sicily. And say thou, too, O herald, that I, Berard, Archbishop of Bari, and Legate of our lord the Pope, do at his command now cut off and excommunicate Otho of Brunswick from the fellowship of all true men and the protection of the Church!"

Otho, deeply enraged at this refusal and denunciation, spurred furiously forward, and his knights laid spears in rest to follow their leader; but the words of excommunication decided the wavering Bishop of Constance to side with the boy sovereign, and he commanded hastily: "Ho, warders; up drawbridge — quick!"

The great chains clanked and tightened, the heavy drawbridge rose in air, and Otho of Brunswick saw the portcullised gate of Constance drop heavily before his very eyes, and knew that his cause was lost.

By just so narrow a chance did young Frederick of Hohenstaufen win his empire.

And now it was won indeed. From every part of Germany came princes, nobles, and knights flocking to the imperial standard. Otho retired to his stronghold in Brunswick; and on the fifth of December, 1212, in the old Römer, or council-house, of Frankfort, five thousand knights with the electors of Germany welcomed the "Boy from Sicily." Four days after, in the great cathedral of Mayence, the pointed arches and rounded dome of which rose high above the storied Rhine, the sad little prince of but five years back was solemnly crowned in presence of a glittering throng, which with cheers of welcome hailed him as Emperor supreme.

And here we leave him. Only seventeen, Frederick of Hohenstaufen — the beggar prince, the friendless orphan of Palermo, after trials and dangers and triumphs stranger than those of any prince of fairy tales or "Arabian Nights" — entered upon a career of empire that has placed him in history as "one of the most remarkable figures of the Middle Ages."

Schooled by the hardships and troubles of his unhappy childhood, the poor little "Child of Apulia" developed into a courageous and energetic youth, and into a man of power and action and imperial renown. Years passed away, and, on the thirteenth of December, 1250, he died at his hunting-lodge of Firenzuola, in his loved Apulian kingdom. A gray old man stood beside the dying monarch's bed — Berard, Archbishop of Palermo and Bari, the only survivor of that dauntless band which, nearly forty years before, had crossed the trackless Alps determined to win Germany or die. The "Boy from Sicily," who had started upon the "quest for his heritage" unheralded and almost unknown, died the most powerful monarch of his day in all the Christian world, unsurpassed in outward splendor, the possessor of six royal crowns — Germany, Burgundy, Lombardy, Sicily, Jerusalem, and the Holy Roman Empire.

A man of magnificent gifts — a great scholar, a far-seeing statesman and law-maker, a valiant and victorious Crusader, a mighty Emperor, but with all the weaknesses and cruel ways that marked the monarchs of those hard old days — this story of his remarkable and romantic boyhood comes down to us as a lesson of triumph over obstacles, showing us, as do so many nobler lives than his, how out of distress and trouble and actual hardships, any boy of energy and spirit may rise to eminence and lofty achievement. The age is passed when kings and princes rise so far above their fellow-men. All may be kings and princes in their special callings if they but have persistent and unflinching determination, and the boy of to-day has it in his power to become, even as did young Frederick of Hohenstaufen, the Boy Emperor, something great in his day and generation — perhaps even be acknowledged, as was he, though from far higher motives, *Stupor Mundi Fredericus* — "Frederick the Wonder of the World!"

FOOTNOTES:

[15] *El Aaziz*, an Arabic phrase for "the excellent" or "most noble one."

[16] Apulia — Southern Italy.

[17] The *Sirocco* is a fierce south-easterly wind of Sicily and the Mediterranean.

VII. Harry Of Monmouth: The Boy General.

(Afterward King Henry the Fifth of England.) A.D. 1402.

A tapestried chamber in the gray old pile known as Berkhampstead Castle. The bright sunlight of an early English spring streaming through the latticed window plays upon the golden head of a fair young maid of ten, who, in a quaint costume of gold-striped taffeta and crimson velvet, looks in evident dismay upon the antics of three merry boys circling around her, as she sits in a carved and high-backed oaken chair. In trim suits of crimson, green, and russet velvet, with curious hanging sleeves and long, pointed shoes, they range themselves before the trembling little maiden, while the eldest lad, a handsome, lithe, and active young fellow of fourteen, sings in lively and rollicking strain:

"Oh, I am King Erik of Denmark,
Tarran, tarran, tarra!
Oh, I am King Erik of Denmark,
Tarran, tarran, tarra!
Oh, I am King Erik of Denmark shore —
A frosty and crusty old Blunderbore —
With ships and knights a-sailing o'er,
To carry Philippa to Elsinore!"

And then with a rousing shout the three boys swooped down upon the beleaguered little damsel and dragged her off to the dim stone staircase that led to the square tower of the keep.

"Have done, have done, Harry," pleaded the little girl as she escaped from her captors. "Master Lionel, thou surely shouldst defend a princess in distress."

"Ay, Princess, but our tutor, Master Rothwell, says that I am to obey my Liege and Prince, and him alone," protested gay young Lionel, "and sure he bade me play the trumpeter of King Erik."

"A plague on King Erik," cried Philippa, seeking refuge behind the high-backed chair. "I wish I had ne'er heard of him and his kingdom of Denmark. O Harry! nurse Joanna tells me that they do eat but frozen turnips and salted beef in his dreadful country, and that the queen-mother, Margaret, wears a gambison [18] and hauberk [19] like to a belted knight."

"Why, of course she does," assented the mischievous Harry; and, drawing a solemn face he added: "Yes — and she eats a little girl, boiled with lentils, every saint's day as a penance. That's why they want an English wife for Erik, for, seest thou, there are so many saints' days that there are not left in Denmark wee damsels enough for the queen's penance."

But the sight of pretty Philippa's woful tears stayed her brother's teasing.

"There, there," he said, soothingly; "never mind my fun, Philippa. This Erik is not so bad a knight I'll warrant me, and when thou art Queen of Denmark, why, I shall be King of England, and my trumpeter, Sir Lionel here, shall sound a gallant defiance as I come

"'Sailing the sea to Denmark shore
With squires and bowmen a hundred score,
If ever this frosty old Blunderbore
Foul treateth Philippa at Elsinore,'

and thus will we gallop away with the rescued queen," he added, as seizing Philippa in his arms he dashed around the room followed by his companions. But while the four were celebrating, in a wild dance of "all hands around," the fancied rescue of the misused queen, the tapestry parted and Sir Hugh de Waterton, the governor of the king's children, entered.

"My lord Prince," he said, "the king thy father craves thy presence in the council-room."

"So; I am summoned," said the Prince; "good Sir Hugh, I will to the king at once. That means 'good-by,' Sis; for to-morrow I am off to the Welsh wars to dance with the lords-marchers and Owen Glendower, to a far different strain. Yield not to these leaguering Danes, Philippa, but if thou dost, when I am back from the Welsh wars, I'll hie me over sea

"'With golden nobles in goodly store
To ransom Philippa at Elsinore,'"

and, kissing his sister fondly, Harry of Monmouth, Prince of Wales, parted the heavy arras and descended to the council-room.

And now the scene changes. Months have passed since that jolly romp in the old castle, among the hills of Hertfordshire, and under a wet and angry sky we stand within the king's tent, glad to escape from the driving storm.

To young Lionel Langley, as he peeped through the outer curtains of the tent and watched the floods of rain, it seemed as if all the mountains in the shires of Brecon and Radnor had turned themselves into water-spouts to drench and drown the camp of the English invaders, as it lay soaked and shivering there in the marches [20] of Wales. King Henry's tent, we learn from an old chronicle, was "picchid on a fayre playne," but Lionel thought it any thing but fair as he turned from the dismal prospect.

"Rain, rain, rain," he grumbled, throwing himself down by the side of stout Humfrey Wallys, archer in the king's guard; "why doth it always rain in this fateful country? Why can it not blow over? Why, — why must we stay cooped up under these soaking tent-tops, with ne'er a sight of fun or fighting?"

"Ah, why, why, why?" said the good-natured archer, "'t is ever why? with thee, Sir Questioner. But, if thou be riddling, ask us something easier. Why doth a cow lie down? Why is it fool's fun to give alms to a blind man? How many calves' tails doth it take to reach to the moon?"

"H'm," grunted Lionel, "thy riddles be as stale as Michaelmas mutton. I can answer them all."

"So — canst thou, young shuttle-brain?" cried the archer, "then, by the mass, thou shalt. Answer now, answer," he demanded, as he tripped up young Lionel's feet and pinned him to the ground with a pikestaff, "answer, or I will wash thy knowing face in my sack-leavings. Why doth a cow lie down?"

"Faith, because she cannot sit," lazily answered Lionel.

"Hear the lad! He doth know it, really. Well — why is it not wise to give alms to a blind man?" demanded Humfrey.

"Because," responded the boy, "even if thou didst, he would be glad could he see thee hanged — as would I also!"

"Thou young knave! Now — how many calves' tails will it take to reach the moon?"

"O Humfrey, ease up thy pikestaff, man; I can barely fetch my breath — how many? Why, one, — if it be long enough," and, wriggling from his captor, the nimble Lionel tripped him up in turn, and, in sheer delight at his discomfiture, turned a back somersault and landed almost on the toes of two unhelmeted knights, who came from the inner pavilion of the royal tent.

"Why, how now, young tumble-foot — dost thou take this for a mummer's booth, that thou dost play thy pranks so closely to thy betters?" a quick voice demanded, and in much shame and confusion Lionel withdrew himself hastily from the royal feet of his "most dread sovereign and lord," King Henry the Fourth, of England.

"Pardon, my Liege," he stammered, "I did but think to stretch my stiffened legs."

"So; thou art tent-weary, too," said the king; and then asked: "And where learn'dst thou that hand-spring?"

"So please your Majesty, from my lord Prince," the boy replied.

"Ay, that thou didst, I'll warrant me," said the king, good-humoredly. "In aught of prank or play, or tumbler's trick, 't is safe to look to young Harry of Monmouth as our pages' sponsor. But where lags the lad, think you, my lord?" he asked, turning to his companion, the Earl of Westmoreland. "We should, methinks, have had post from him ere this."

"'T is this fearful weather stays the news, your Majesty," replied the earl. "No courserman could pass the Berwyn and

Plinlimmon hills in so wild a storm."

"Ay, wild indeed," said the king, peering out through the parted curtains. "I am fain almost to believe these men of Wales, who vaunt that the false Glendower is a black necromancer who can call to his aid the dread demons of the air. Hark to that blast," he added, as a great gust of wind shook the royal tent. "'T is like a knight's defiance, and, like true knights, let us answer it. Hollo, young Lionel, be thou warder of thy king, and sound an answering blast."

Lionel, who was blest with the strong lungs of healthy boyhood, grasped the trumpet, and a defiant peal rang through the royal tent. But it was an unequal contest, for instantly, as chronicles old Capgrave, "there blew suddenly so much wynd, and so impetuous, with a gret rain, that the Kyng's tent was felled, and a spere cast so violently, that, an the Kyng had not been armed, he had been ded of the strok."

From all sides came the rush of help, and the king and his attendants were soon rescued, unharmed from the fallen pavilion. But Humfrey, the stout old archer, muttered, as he rubbed his well-thumped pate: "Good sooth, 't is, truly, the art magic of Glendower himself. It payeth not to trifle with malignant spirits. Give me to front an honest foe, and not these hidden demons of the air."

As if satisfied with its victory over a mortal king, the fury of the storm abated, and that afternoon Lionel entered the royal presence with the announcement: "Tidings, my lord King; tidings from the noble Prince of Wales! a courier waits without."

"Bid him enter," said the king, and, all bespattered and dripping from his ride through the tempest, the courier entered and, dropping on his knee, presented the king a writing from the prince.

"At last!" said Henry, as he hastily scanned the note; "a rift in these gloomy clouds. Break we our camp, my lord Westmoreland, and back to Hereford town. We do but spend our strength to little use awaiting a wily foe in these flooded plains. This billet tells me that Sir Harry Percy and my lord of Worcester, with our son the Prince, have cooped up the rebels in the Castle of Conway, and that Glendower himself is in the Snowdon Hills. As for thee, young Sir Harlequin," he added, turning to Lionel, "if thou wouldst try thy mettle in other ways than in tumbler's tricks and in defiance of the wind, thou mayst go with Sir Walter Blount to thy tutor, the Prince, and the Welsh wars in the north."

Next day, the camp was broken up, and, in high spirits, Lionel, with the small company of knights and archers detached for service in the north, left the southern marches for the camp of the prince.

It was the year of grace 1402. Henry of Lancaster, usurping the crown and power of the unfortunate King Richard II., ruled now as Henry IV., "by the grace of God, King of England and of France and Lord of Ireland." But "uneasy lies the head that wears a crown," and, king though he was — "Most Excellent, Most Dread, and Most Sovereign Lord," as his subjects addressed him — he was lord and sovereign over a troubled and distracted realm. Scotland, thronging the Lowlands, poured her bonnets and pikes across the northern border; France, an ever-watchful enemy, menaced the slender possessions in Calais and Aquitaine; traitors at home plotted against the life of the king; and the men of Wales, rallying to the standard of their countryman, Owen Glendower, who styled himself the Prince of Wales, forced the English to unequal and disadvantageous battle among their hills and valleys. So the journey of Lionel to the north was a careful and cautious one; and, constantly on their guard against ambushes, surprises, and sudden assaults, the little band of archers and men-at-arms among whom he rode pushed their watchful way toward the Vale of Conway. They were just skirting the easterly base of the Snowdon Hills, where, three thousand feet above them, the rugged mountain peaks look down upon the broad and beautiful Vale of Conway, when a noise of crackling branches ahead startled the wary archer, Wallys, and he said to Lionel:

"Look to thine arms, lad; there may be danger here. But no," he added, as the "view halloo" of the hunters rose in air, "'t is but the merry chase. Hold here, and let us see the sport."

Almost as he spoke, there burst from the thicket, not a hundred yards away, a splendid red deer, whose spreading antlers proclaimed him to be a "stag of twelve" or "stag-royal." Fast after him dashed the excited hunters; but, leading them all, spurred a sturdy young fellow of eager fifteen — tall and slender, but quick and active in every movement, as he yielded himself to the free action of his horse and cheered on the hounds. The excitement was contagious, and Lionel, spite of the caution of his friend the archer, could not restrain himself. His "view halloo" was shouted with boyish impetuosity as, fast at the heels of the other young hunter, he spurred his willing horse. But now the deer turned to the right and made for a distant thicket, and Lionel saw the young hunter spring from his lagging steed, and, with a stout cord reeled around his arm, dash after the stag afoot, while hounds and hunters panted far behind.

It was a splendid race of boy and beast. The lad's quick feet seemed scarcely to touch the ground, every spring bringing him nearer and nearer to his noble prey. There is a final spurt; the coil of cord flies from the hunter's arm, as his quick fling sends it straight in air; the noose settles over the broad antlers of the buck; the youth draws back with a sudden but steady jerk, and the defeated deer drops to earth, a doomed and panting captive.

"There is but one lad in all England can do that!" cried enthusiastic Lionel, as with a loud huzza, he spurred toward the spot so as to be "in at the death."

"Lend me thy knife, page," the boy hunter demanded, as Lionel sprang from his horse, "mine I think hath leaped from my belt into yonder pool."

Flash! gleamed the sharp steel in air; deep to the hilt it plunged into the victim's throat, and, kneeling on the body of the dying stag, Harry of Monmouth, Prince of Wales, the fleetest and most fearless of England's youthful hunters, looked up into Lionel's admiring face.

"Hey O!" he cried. "Sure, 't is Lionel Langley! Why, how far'st thou, lad, and how cam'st thou here?"

"I come, my Lord," Lionel replied, "with Sir Walter Blount's following of squires and archers, whom his Majesty, the King, hath sent to thy succour."

"You are right welcome all," said Prince Harry, "and you come in good stead, for sure we need your aid. But wind this horn of mine, Lionel, and call in the hunt." And as Lionel's notes sounded loud and clear, the rest of the chase galloped up, and soon the combined trains rode on to the English camp in the Vale of Conway.

There, in the train of Prince Harry, Lionel passed the winter and spring; while his young leader, then scarce sixteen, led his hardy troops, a miniature army of scarce three thousand men, up and down the eastern marches of Wales, scouring the country from Conway Castle to Harlech Hold, and from the Irish Sea to Snowden and to Shrewsbury gates. The battles fought were little more than forays and skirmishes, — the retaliations of fire and sword, now in English fields and now on Welsh borders; but it was a good "school of the soldier," in which Lionel learned the art of war, and Harry of Monmouth bore himself right gallantly.

But greater troubles were brewing, and braver deeds in store. On a fair July morning in the year 1403, Lionel, who now served the prince as squire of the body, entering his pavilion hastily, said, in much excitement:

"My Lord, my Lord, the Earl of Worcester has gone!"

"Gone?" echoed the prince. "What dost thou mean? Gone? When — where — how?"

"None know, my Lord," Lionel replied. "This morning his pavilion was found deserted, and with him are fled Sir Herbert Tressell, and the squires and archers of my lord of Worcester's train."

Now, the Earl of Worcester was the "tutor," or guardian, of the prince, a trusted noble of the House of Percy, and appointed by the king to have the oversight or guidance of young Harry; and his sudden flight from camp greatly surprised the prince.

"My lord Prince," said Sir Walter Blount, entering as hastily as had Lionel, "here is a courier from the worshipful Constable of Chester, with secret tidings that the Percies are in arms against my lord the king."

"The Percies up, and my lord of Worcester fled?" exclaimed the prince. "This bodes no good for us. Quick, get thee to horse, Lionel. Speed like the wind to Shrewsbury. Get thee fair escort from my lord of Warwick, and then on to the king at Burton." And in less than ten minutes Lionel was a-horse, bearing the prince's billet that told the doleful news of the new rebellion, spurring fast to Shrewsbury and the King.

Before three days had passed the whole great plot was known, and men shook their heads in dismay and doubt at the tidings that the great houses of Percy and of Mortimer, rebelling against the king for both real and fancied grievances, had made a solemn league with the Welsh rebel, Owen Glendower, to dethrone King Henry, whom the Percies themselves had helped to the throne. A fast-growing army, led by the brave Sir Henry Percy, — whom men called Hotspur, from his mighty valor and his impetuous temper, — and by the Earl of Douglas, most valiant of the Scottish knights, was even now marching upon Shrewsbury to raise the standard of revolt.

"Hotspur a rebel? Worcester a traitor?" exclaimed the king in amazement, as he read Lionel's tidings. "Whom may we trust if these be false?"

But Henry the Fourth of England was not one to delay in action, nor to "cry over spilled milk." His first surprise over, he sent a fleet courier to London announcing the rebellion to his council, but bravely assuring them for their consolation that he was "powerful enough to conquer all his enemies." Then he gave orders to break the camp at Burton and march on Shrewsbury direct; and, early next morning, Lionel was spurring back to his boy general, Prince Harry, with orders from the king to meet him at once with all his following at Bridgenorth Castle.

So, down from the east marches of Wales to Bridgenorth towers came Prince Harry speedily, with his little army of trusty knights and squires, stalwart archers and men-at-arms, — hardy fighters all, trained to service in the forays of the rude Welsh wars, in which, too, their gallant young commander had himself learned coolness, caution, strategy, and unshrinking valor — the chief attributes of successful leadership.

Where Bridgenorth town stands upon the sloping banks of Severn, "like to old Jerusalem for pleasant situation," as the pilgrim travellers reported, there rallied in those bright summer days of 1403 a hastily summoned army for the "putting down of the rebel Percies." With waving banners and with gleaming lances, with the clank of heavy armor and ponderous engines of war, with the royal standard borne by Sir Walter Blount and his squires, out through the "one mighty gate" of Bridgenorth Castle passed the princely leaders, marshalling their army of fourteen thousand men across the broad plain of Salop toward the towers and battlements of the beleaguered town of Shrewsbury.

The king himself led the right wing, and young Harry of Monmouth, Prince of Wales, the left. So rapidly did the royal captains move, that the impetuous Hotspur, camped under the walls of the stout old castle, only knew of their near approach when, on the morning of July 20th, he saw upon the crest of a neighboring hill the waving banners of King Henry's host. The gates of Shrewsbury opened to the king, and across the walls of the ancient town royalist and rebel faced each other, armed for bloody fight.

Lionel's young heart beat high as he watched the warlike preparations, and, glancing across to where near Haughmond Abbey floated the rebel standard, he found himself humming one of the rough old war tunes he had learned in Wales:

"Oh, we hope to do thee a gleeful thing
With a rope, a ladder, and eke a ring;
On a gallows high shalt thou swing full free —
And thus shall the ending of traitors be."

"Nay, nay, Lionel, be not so sure of that," said the prince, as he, too, caught up the spirited air. "Who faces Hotspur and Douglas, as must we, will be wise not to talk rope and gallows till he sees the end of the affair. But come to the base-court. I'll play thee a rare game of — hark, though," he said, as a loud trumpet-peal sounded beyond the walls, "there goeth the rebel defiance at the north gate. Come, attend me to the king's quarters, Lionel." And hastening across the inner court of the castle, the two lads entered the great guard-room just as the warders ushered into the king's presence the knights who, in accordance with the laws of battle, bore to the king the defiance of his enemies.

"Henry of Hereford and Lancaster!" said the herald, flinging a steel gauntlet on the floor with a ringing clash, "there lieth my lord of Percy's gage! thus doth he defy thee to battle!"

The Prince Harry, with the flush of excitement on his fair young face, sprang from his father's side and picked up the gage of battle. "This shall be my duty," he said, and then the herald read before the king the paper containing the manifesto, or "defiance," of the Percies.

Prince Henry Picks Up The Gage Of The Percies' Defiance. — "This Shall Be My Duty," He Said.

In spirited articles the missive accused the king of many wrongs and oppressions, each article closing with the sentence: "Wherefore, thou art forsworn and false," while the following hot and ringing words concluded the curious paper: "For the which cause, we defy thee, thy fautores, [21] and complices, as common traytoures and destroyers of the realme and the invadours, oppressors, and confounders of the verie true and right heires to the crown of England, which thynge we intende with our handes to prove this daie, Almighty God helping us."

The king took the paper from the herald's hand and simply said:

"Withdraw, sir herald, and assure your lord that we will reply to him with the sword, and prove in battle his quarrel to be false and traitorous and feigned."

And then the herald withdrew, courteously escorted; but it is said that King Henry, saddened at the thought of the valiant English blood that must be shed, sent, soon after, gentle words and offers of pardon to the Percies if they would return to their allegiance — all of which the Earl of Worcester, envious of the king, misreported to his generous but hot-headed nephew, Sir Harry Percy. So wrong a message did the false earl give, that both Hotspur and the Douglas flamed with rage, and without waiting for Owen Glendower's forces and the expected reënforcements from the north, gave orders for instant battle, thus hastening the conflict before they were really ready. "The more haste, the less speed" is a strong old adage, boys, that holds good both in peace and war, and bitterly was it repented of on that "sad and sorry field of Shrewsbury."

So, out through the north gate of Shrewsbury, on a Friday afternoon, swept the army of the king, fourteen thousand strong, and, back from the abbey foregate and the Severn's banks, dropped the Percies' host, thirteen thousand banded English, Scotch, and Welsh. In a space of open, rolling country known as Hately Field — fit name for a place of battle between former friends, — three miles from Shrewsbury town, the rival armies pitched their tents, drew their battle lines, and waited for the dawn.

It is the morning of Saturday, the twenty-second of July, 1403. Both camps are astir, and in the gray light that precedes the dawn the preparation for battle is made. The sun lights up the alder-covered hills, the trumpet sounds to arms, the standards sway, the burnished armor gleams and rings as knights and squires fall into their appointed places; the cloth-yard shafts are fitted to the archer's bows, and then, up from a sloping field, sweet with the odor of the pea-blossoms that cover it, there comes in loud defiance the well-known war-cry of the Percies: "*Esperance, esperance!* Percy, ho, a Percy!" and Hotspur with his Northumbrian archers sweeps to the attack amidst a terrible flight of arrows and of spears.

"Play up, sir trumpeter!" shouted Harry of Monmouth, rising in his stirrups. "Play up your answering blast. Shake out our standard free. Now, forward all! Death to traitors! St. George — St. George for England!"

"St. George for England!" came the answering echo from King Henry's line; "*Esperance*, Percy!" sounded again from the rebel ranks, and "in a place called Bullfield," both armies closed in conflict.

"So furiously, the armies joined," runs the old chronicle: "the arrows fell as fall the leaves on the ground after a frosty night at the approach of winter. There was no room for the arrows to reach the ground; every one struck a mortal man." The first attack was against the king's own ranks. Hotspur, with his Northumbrian arrows, and Douglas, with his Scottish spears, pressed hotly upon them, while Worcester's Cheshire archers from a slope near by sent their whizzing messengers straight into the king's lines. Though answering valiantly, the terrible assault was too severe for the king's men. They wavered, staggered, swayed, and broke — a ringing cheer went up from the enemy, when, just at the critical moment, with an "indignant onset," Harry of Monmouth dashed to his father's aid. His resistless rush changed the tide of battle, and the king's line was saved.

A sorry record is the story of that fearful fight. For three long hours the battle raged from Haughmond Abbey on to Berwick Bridge, and ere the noon of that bloody day, twelve thousand valiant Englishmen fell on the fatal field. "So faute thei, to gret harm of this nacion," says one queer old chronicle; and another says: "It was more to be noted vengeable, for there the father was slain of the son and the son of the father." The great historian

Hume tells us that "We shall scarcely find any battle in those ages where the shock was more terrible and more constant."

The fire of passion and of fight spread even to the youngest page and squire, and as Lionel pressed close after the "gilded helmet and the three-plumed crest" of his brilliant young prince, his face flamed with the excitement of the battle-hour. Again and again he saw the king unhorsed and fighting desperately for his crown and life; again and again he saw the fiery Hotspur and Douglas, the Scot, charge furiously on the king they had sworn to kill. Backward and forward the tide of battle rolls; now royalist, now rebel seems the victor. Hark! What shout is that?

"The king, the king is down!"

And where Hotspur and the Douglas fight around the hillock now known as the "King's Croft," Lionel misses the golden crest, he misses the royal banner of England!

"Sir Walter Blount is killed! the standard is lost!" is now the sorry cry.

But now the prince and his hardy Welsh fighters charge to the rescue, and Lionel gave a cry of terror as he saw a whizzing arrow tear into the face of his beloved prince. Young Harry reeled with his hurt, and Lionel with other gentlemen of the guard caught him in their arms. There was confusion and dismay.

"The prince is hurt!" cried Lionel, and almost as an echo rose those other shouts:

"The king is slain!"

"Long live the Percy!"

"Back to the rear, my lord!" pleaded Lionel, as he wiped the blood from the fair young face of the prince.

"Back, back, my lord Prince. Back to my tent," urged the Earl of Westmoreland, and "Back, back, while there is yet safety," said the other knights, as the tide of battle surged toward the bleeding prince.

"Stand off!" cried young Harry, springing to his feet. "Stand off; my lords! Far be from me such disgrace as that, like a poltroon, I should stain my arms by flight. If the prince flies, who will wait to end the battle?"

And just then another shout arose — a joyous, ringing cry:

"Ho, the king lives! the standard is safe! St. George for England!" And the brave young Harry, turning to his guard, said:

"What, my lords? to be carried back before the victory? 'T would be to me a perpetual death! Lead me, I implore you, to the very face of the foe. I may not say to my friends: 'Go ye on first to the fight!' Be it mine to say: 'Follow me, my friends!'"

Then, as the royal standard waved once more aloft, he burst with his followers into the thick of the fight, his unyielding valor giving new strength to all.

And now the end is near. An archer's arrow, with unerring aim, pierces the valiant Hotspur, and he falls dead upon the field.

"Harry Percy is dead! Victory, victory! St. George and victory!" rings the cry from thousands of the loyal troops, and, like a whirlwind, a panic of fear seizes the rebel ranks. Douglas is a prisoner; the Earl of Worcester surrenders; the rout is general.

"Then fled thei that myte fle," says the chronicle, or, as Hall, another of the old chroniclers records: "The Scots fled, the Welshmen ran, the traitors were overcome; then neither woods hindered nor hills stopped the fearful hearts of them that were vanquished."

So ended the "sad and sorry field of Shrewsbury," a fitting prelude to that bloody era of strife known as the Wars of the Roses, which, commencing in the sad reign of the son of this boy general, Harry of Monmouth, was to stain England with the blood of Englishmen through fifty years.

And now the dust and roar of battle die away, and we find ourselves amidst the Christmas-tide revels in royal Windsor, where, in one of the lordly apartments, our friend Lionel, like a right courtly young squire, is paying duteous attention to his liege lady, the fair Princess Philippa. As we draw near the pair, we catch the words of the princess, now a mature and stately young damsel of twelve, as she says to Lionel, who, gorgeous in a suit of motley velvet, listens respectfully:

"And let me tell thee, Master Lionel, that, from all I can make of good Master Lucke's tedious Latin letters, King Erik is a right noble prince, and a husband meet and fit for a Princess of England."

"Oh, ho! sits the wind in that quarter?" a gay voice exclaims, and Prince Harry comes to his sister's side. "Well, here be I in a pretty mess. Was I not prepared to deny in council, before all the lords, this petition of King Erik for our Princess, — ay, and to back it up with my stout bowmen from the marches? Beshrew me, Sis, but since when didst thou shift to so fair a taste for — what was it? frozen turnips and salted beef? And — how is the queen-mother's appetite?"

But with a dignified little shrug, the princess disdains her brother's banter, and the merry prince goes on to say:

"Well, I must use my ready bows and lances somewhere, and if not to right the wrongs of the fair Philippa against this frosty and crusty — pardon me, your Highness, this *right noble* King Erik of Denmark, — then against that other 'most dread and sovereign lord, Owen, Prince of Wales,' as he doth style himself. To-morrow will this betrothal be signed; and then, Lionel, hey for the southern marches and the hills and heaths of Wales!"

So, amidst siege and skirmish and fierce assault the winter passed away, and grew to spring again; and so well and vigilantly did this boy leader defend the borders of his principality against the forays of Glendower's troops, that we find the gentry of the county of Hereford petitioning the king to publicly thank "our dear and honored Lord and Prince, your son," for his "defence and governance of this your county of Hereford." And, out of all the vigilance and worry, the dash and danger of this exciting life, Harry of Monmouth was learning those lessons of patience, fortitude, coolness, self-denial, and valor that enabled him, when barely twenty-eight, to win the mighty fight at Agincourt, and to gain the proud title of Henry the Victorious. For war, despite its horrors and terrors, has ever been a great and absorbing game, in which he who is most skilful, most cautious, and most fearless, makes the winning moves.

"Tidings, tidings, my lord Prince!" came the message from one hard-riding courserman, as his foam-flecked steed dashed through the great gate of the castle of Hereford. "My lord of Warwick hath met your Welsh rebels near the Red Castle by Llyn Du, and hath routed them with much loss." But a few days later, came another horseman with the words: "Tidings, tidings, my lord Prince! Sir William Newport hath been set upon at Craig y Dorth by your rebels of Wales, 'with myty hand,' and so sore was his strait that he hath fled into Monmouth town, while many gallant gentlemen and archers lie dead of their hurt, by the great stones of Treleg."

"Sir William routed?" exclaimed the prince, "'t is ours, then, to succor him. Lionel, summon Lord Talbot." That sturdy old fighter was soon at hand. "Fare we to Monmouth straight, my lord," said the prince. Here is sorry news, but we will right the day."

Very speedily the little army of the prince was on the move along the lovely valley of the Wye; and, on the tenth of March, 1405, they were lodged within the red walls of that same great castle of Monmouth, "in the which," says the old chronicle, "it pleased God to give life to the noble King Henry V., who of the same is called Harry of Monmouth."

"Tidings, tidings, my lord Prince," came the report of the scouts; "the false traitor, Glendower, with your rebels of Glamorgan and Usk, of Netherwent and Overwent, have lodged themselves, to the number of eight thousand, in your town of Grosmont, scarce six miles away."

Eight thousand strong! and Prince Harry had with him barely five thousand men. But with the morning sun the order "Banners advance!" was given, and the fearless young general of seventeen drew his little army along the banks of the winding Monnow to the smoking ruins of the plundered town of Grosmont.

But the difference in numbers did seem a serious obstacle to success.

"Is it wise, my lord Prince," cautioned Lord Talbot, "to pit ourselves bodily against so strong a power? They be eight thousand strong and count us nearly two to one."

"Very true, my lord," said the intrepid prince, "but victory lieth not in a multitude of people, but in the power of God. Let us help to prove it here, and by the aid of Heaven and our good right arms, may we this day win the unequal fight!"

"Amen!" said Lord Talbot; "none welcome the day and duty more than I."

Out from the castle on its lofty rock and forth from the smoking ruins of the town swarmed the men of Wales confident of easy victory. The armies of the rival princes of Wales stood face to face. Then the trumpets sounded; the red cross of St. George and the odd-looking banner of the Trinity fluttered above the English ranks; stout Lord Talbot rode before the lines and tossing his truncheon in air shouted: "Now — strike!" There is a sudden rush, and as the battle-cries "St. George and England!" "St. David for Wales!" rise in air the opposing armies join in deadly fight. Short, but stubborn and bloody was the conflict. Victory rested with the little army of Prince Harry, and before the sun went down Glendower and his routed forces were in full retreat, leaving a thousand sturdy Welshmen dead upon the field.

Following up his victory with quick and determined action, the boy general hurried at the heels of Glendower's broken ranks, and on Sunday, the fifteenth of March, 1405, faced them again under the old towers of the castle of Usk. Swift and sudden fell his attack. The Welsh ranks broke before the fury of his onset, and, with over fifteen hundred lost in killed or prisoners, with his brother Tudor slain and his son Gruffyd a captive in the hands of the English, Owen Glendower fled with the remnant of his defeated army into the grim fastnesses of the Black Hills of Brecon.

It was a sad day for Wales, for it broke the power and sway of their remarkable and patriotic leader, Glendower, and made them, erelong, vassals of the English crown. But the bells of London rang loud and merrily when, three days after the fight, a rapid courserman spurred through the city gates, bearing to the council a copy of the modest letter in which the young general announced his victory to his "most redoubted and most sovereign lord and father," the king.

Lionel, close in attendance on his much-loved leader, followed him through all the troubles and triumphs of the Welsh wars; followed him when, a few months after, before the gates of Worcester, the French allies of the Welsh rebels were driven from the kingdom; and followed him, "well and bravely appareled," when, in May, 1406, the king, with a brilliant company of lords and ladies, gathered at the port of Lynn to bid farewell to the young Princess Philippa, as she sailed with the Danish ambassadors, "in great state," over the sea, "to be joyned in wedlok" to King Erik of Denmark.

And here we must leave our gallant young prince. A boy no longer, his story is now that of a wise and vigorous young manhood, which, in prince and king, bore out the promise of his boyish days. Dying at thirty-five — still a young man — he closed a career that stands on record as a notable one in the annals of the world.

But when you come to read in Shakespeare's matchless verse the plays of "King Henry IV." and "King Henry V.," do not, in your delight over his splendid word-pictures, permit yourself to place too strong a belief in his portrait of young "Prince Hal," and his scrapes and follies and wild carousals with fat old Falstaff and his boon companions. For the facts of history now prove the great poet mistaken; and "Prince Hal," though full of life and spirit, fond of pleasure and mischief, and, sometimes, of rough and thoughtless fun, stands on record as a valiant, high-minded, clear-hearted, and conscientious lad. "And when we reflect," says one of his biographers, "to what a high station he had been called whilst yet a boy; with what important commissions he had been intrusted; how much fortune seems to have done to spoil him by pride and vain-glory from his earliest youth, this page of our national records seems to set him high among the princes of the world; not so much as an undaunted warrior and triumphant hero, as the conqueror of himself, the example of a chastened, modest spirit, of filial reverence, and of a single mind bent on his duty."

The conqueror of himself! It was this that gave him grace to say, when crowned King of England in Westminster: "The first act of my reign shall be to pardon all who have offended me; and I pray God that if He foresees I am like to be any other than a just and good king, He may be pleased to take me from the world rather than seat me on a throne to live a public calamity to my country." It was this that gave him his magnificent courage at Agincourt, where, with barely six thousand Englishmen, he faced and utterly routed a French host of nearly sixty thousand men; it was this that, in the midst of the gorgeous pageant which welcomed him at London as the hero of Agincourt, made him refuse to allow his battle-bruised helmet and his dinted armor to be displayed as trophies of his valor. It was this that kept him brave, modest, and high-minded through all the glories and successes of his short but eventful life, that made him the idol of the people and one of the most brilliant figures in the crowded pages of English history.

It is not given to us, boys and girls, to be royal in name, but we may be royal in nature, even as was Harry of Monmouth, the brilliant young English prince, and, knowing now something of his character, we can understand the loving loyalty of a devoted people that marks this entry of his death as it stands in the "Acts of Privy Council," the official record of the public doings of his realm:

"Departed this life at the Castle of Bois de Vincennes, near Paris, on the last day of August, in the year 1422, and the tenth of his reign, the most Christian Champion of the Church, the Bright Beam of Wisdom, the Mirror of Justice, the Unconquered King, the Flower and Pride of all Chivalry — Henry the Fifth, King of England, Heir and Regent of France, and Lord of Ireland."

FOOTNOTES:

[18] A stuffed doublet worn under armor.

[19] A coat of mail formed of small steel rings interwoven.

[20] The "marches" — frontiers or boundaries of a country. The nobles who held fiefs or castles in such border-lands were called "the lords-marchers."

[21] Favorers, or abettors.

VIII. GIOVANNI OF FLORENCE, THE BOY CARDINAL.

(Afterward Pope Leo the Tenth.) A.D. 1490.

It was one of the wild carnival days of 1490. From the great Gate of San Gallo to the quaint old Bridge of the Goldsmiths, the fair city of Florence blazed with light and rang with shout and song. A struggling mass of spectators surged about the noble palace of the Medici, as out through its open gate-way and up the broad street known as the Via Larga streamed the great carnival pageant of Lorenzo the Magnificent, the head of the house of Medici.

"Room for the noble Abbot of Passignano! room for my Lord Cardinal!" shouted a fresh young voice from the head of the grand staircase that led from the *loggia* of the palace to the great entrance-hall below.

"So; say'st thou thus, Giulio?" another boyish voice exclaimed. "Then will I, too, play the herald for thee. Room," he cried, "for the worthy Prior of Capua! room for the noble Knight of St. John!" And down the broad staircase, thronged with gallant costumes, brilliant banners, and gleaming lances, the two merry boys elbowed their way.

Boys? you ask. Yes, boys — both of them, for all their priestly and high-sounding titles. In those far-off days, as we shall see, honors were distributed not so much for merit as from policy; and when royalty married royalty at ten and twelve to serve the ends of state, there was nothing so very wonderful in a noble prior of eleven or a lord cardinal of thirteen.

"Well, well, my modest young Florentines," said Lorenzo de Medici, in his harsh but not unkindly voice, as he met the boys in the grand and splendidly decorated entrance-hall; "if ye do but make your ways in life with such determination as that, all offices needs must yield to you. A truce to tattle, though, my fair Giulio. Modesty best becomes the young; Giovanni's cardinalate, remember, has not yet been proclaimed, and 't is wisest to hold our tongues till we may wag them truthfully. But, come," he added in a livelier tone, "to horse, to horse! the Triumph waits for none, —

noble abbot and worshipful knight though they be — like to your shining selves. To-night be ye boys only. Ho, for fun and frolic; down with care and trouble! Sing it out, sing it out, my boys, well and lustily:

"Dance and carol every one
Of our band so bright and gay;
See your sweethearts how they run
Through the jousts for you to-day."

And with this glee from one of his own gay carnival songs, Lorenzo the Magnificent sprang to the back of his noble Barbary horse, Morello, and spurred forward to mingle in the glories of the pageant.

It was a wondrous display — this carnival pageant, or "Triumph," of the Medici. Great golden cars, richly decorated, and drawn by curious beasts; horses dressed in the skins of lions and tigers and elephants; shaggy buffaloes and timorous giraffes from the Medicean villa at Careggi; fantastic monsters made up of mingled men and boys and horses, with other surprising figures as riders; dragons and dwarfs, giants and genii; beautiful young girls and boys dressed in antique costumes to represent goddesses and divinities of the old mythologies; and a chubby little gilded boy, seated on a great globe and representing the Golden Age — the age of every thing beautiful in art and life; — these and many other attractions made up the glittering display which, accompanied by Lorenzo the Magnificent and his retinue of over five hundred persons, "mounted, masked, and bravely apparelled," and gleaming in the light of four hundred flaring torches, traversed the streets of Florence, "singing in many voices all sorts of *canzones*, madrigals, and popular songs."

"By the stone nose of the *marzoccho*, [22] but this is more joyous than the droning tasks we left behind us at Pisa; is it not, my Giovanni?" gayly exclaimed the younger of the two boys as, glittering in a suit of crimson velvet and cloth of gold, he rode in advance of one of the great triumphal cars. "My faith," he continued, "what would grim-eyed old Fra Bartolommeo say could he see thee, his choicest pupil in pontifical law, masking in a violet velvet suit and a gold-brocaded vest?"

"I fear me, Giulio," replied his cousin Giovanni, a pleasant-looking, brown-faced lad of nearly fourteen, "I fear me the good Fra would pull a long and chiding face at *both* our brave displays. You know how he can look when he takes us to task? And tall? Why, he seems always to grow as high as Giotto's tower there."

"Say, rather, like to the leaning tower in his own Pisa! for he seems as tall, and threatens to come down full as sure and heavily upon us poor unfortunates! Ah, yes, I know how he looks, Giovanni; he tries it upon me full often!" and Giulio's laugh of recollection was tempered with feeling memories.

Here an older boy, a brisk young fellow of sixteen, in a shining suit of silver and crimson brocade, rode toward them.

"Messer Giovanni," he said, "what say'st thou to dropping out of the triumph here by the Vecchio Palace? Then may we go back by the Via Pinti and see the *capannucci*."

Now, the *capannucci* was one of the peculiar carnival institutions of the Florentine boys of old, as dear to their hearts as are the fifth of November and its 'Guy' to the young Londoner of to-day. A great tree would be dragged into the centre of some broad street or square by a crowd of ready youngsters. There it would be set upright and propped or steadied by great faggots and pieces of wood. This base would then be fired, and as the blaze flamed from the faggots or crept up the tall tree-trunk, all the yelling boys danced in the flaring light. Then, when the *capannucci* fell with a great crash, the terrible young Florentine urchins never omitted to wage, over the charred trunk and the glowing embers, a furious rough-and-tumble fight.

Giovanni and Giulio, for all their high-sounding titles, welcomed exciting variety as readily as do any other active and wide-awake boys, and they assented gleefully to the young Buonarotti's suggestion.

"Quick, to the Via Pinti!" they cried, and yielding up their horses to the silver-liveried grooms who attended them, they turned from the pageant, and with their black visors, or half masks, partly drawn, they pushed their way through the crowds that surged under the great bell tower of the Palazzo Vecchio and thronged the gayly decorated street called the Via Pinti.

With a ready handful of *danarini* and *soldi*, small Florentine coins of that day, they easily satisfied the demands of the brown-skinned little street arabs who had laid great pieces of wood, called the *stili*, across the street, and would let none pass until they had yielded to their shrill demand of "Tribute, tribute! a *soldi* for tribute at the *stili* of San Marco!"

With laugh and shout and carnival jest, the three boys were struggling through the crowd toward the rising flame of a distant *capannucci*, when suddenly, with a swish and a thud, there came plump against the face of the young Giovanni one of the thin sugar eggs which, filled with red wine, was one of the favorite carnival missiles. Like a flow of blood the red liquid streamed down the broad, brown cheek of the lad, and streaked his violet tunic. He looked around dismayed.

"Ha, *bestia*!" he cried, as his quick eye detected the successful marksman in a group of laughing young fellows a few rods away. "'T was thou, wast it? Revenge, revenge, my comrades!" and the three lads sent a well-directed volley of return shots that made their assailants duck and dodge for safety. Then followed a frequent carnival scene. The shots and counter-shots drew many lookers-on, and soon the watchers changed to actors. The crowd quickly separated into two parties, the air seemed full of the flying missiles, and, in the glare of the great torches that, held by iron rings, flamed from the corner of a noble palace, the carnival fight raged fast and furiously. In the hottest of the strife a cheer arose as the nimble Giulio, snatching a brilliant crimson scarf from the shoulders of a laughing flower-girl, captured, next, a long pikestaff from a masker of the opposite side. Tying the crimson scarf to the long pike-handle, he charged the enemy, crying, "Ho, forward all!" His supporters followed him with a resistless rush; another volley of carnival ammunition filled the air, and a shout of victory went up as their opponents broke before their charge and the excited crowd went surging up the street. Again a stand was made, again the missiles flew, and now, the candy bon-

bons failing, the reckless combatants kept up the fight with street refuse, — dust and dirt, and even dangerous stones.

It was in one of those hand-to-hand encounters that a tall and supple young fellow dashed from the opposing ranks and grappled with Giulio for the possession of the crimson standard. To and fro the boys swayed and tugged. In sheer defence the less sturdy Giulio struck out at his opponent's face, and down dropped the guarded disguise of the small black visor.

"Ho, an Albizzi!" Giulio exclaimed, as he recognized his antagonist. Then, as the long pikestaff was wrested from his grasp, he raised the well-known cry of his house, "*Palle, Palle!* Medici to the rescue." [23]

"Ha, Medici — is it?" the young Albizzi cried, and, as Giovanni de Medici pressed to the aid of his cousin, Francesco Albizzi clutched at Giovanni's mask in turn and tore it from his face.

"Hollo!" shouted the scornful Albizzi. "We have uncovered the game! Look, boys, 't is Messer Giovanni himself! Hail to My Lord Cardinal! Hail to the young magnifico!" and, doffing his purple bonnet, as if in reverence to Giovanni, he struck the lad with it full on his broad, brown cheek.

His followers applauded his deed with a shout, but it was a weak and spiritless one, for it was scarcely safe to make fun of the Medici then in Florence, and cowards, you know, always take the stronger side.

The supporters of the Medici hastened to wipe out the insult offered to the boy cardinal. They pressed forward to annihilate Albizzi's fast-lessening band, but the young Giovanni interfered.

"Nay, hold, friends," he said, "'t is but a carnival frolic, and 't is ended now. Messer Francesco did but speak in jest, and, sure, I bear no malice."

But the hot-headed Albizzi, the son of a house that had ever been rivals and enemies of the Medici, would listen to no compromise.

"Ho, hark to the smooth-tongued Medici!" he cried. "Boys of

Florence, will ye bow to this baby priest? Your fathers were but boys when they struck for the liberties of Florence and drove *this* fellow's father, the lordly magnifico, like a whipped cur behind the doors of the sacristy, and scattered the blood of *that* boy's father on the very steps of the altar of the Reparata!" [24]

The young Giulio, when he heard this brutal allusion to the murder of his father, could restrain himself no longer; but, rushing at Francesco Albizzi, expended all his fierce young strength upon the older boy in wildly aimed and harmless blows.

Giovanni would have again interceded, but when he saw the vindictive young Albizzi draw a short dagger from his girdle, he felt that the time for words had passed. Springing to the relief of his cousin, he clutched the dagger-arm of the would-be murderer. There was a rallying of adherents on both sides; young faces grew hot with passion, and a bloody street fight seemed certain.

But, hark! Across the strife comes the clash of galloping steel. There is a rush of hurrying feet, a glare of flaming torches, a glimmer of shining lances, and, around from the Via Larga, in a brilliant flash of color, swings the banner of Florence, the great white lily on the blood-red field. Fast behind it presses the well-known escutcheon of the seven golden balls, and the armed servants of the house of Medici sweeps down upon the combatants.

"*Palle, palle!* Medici, ho, a Medici!" rings the shout of rescue. The flashing Milan sword of young Messer Pietro, the elder brother of Giovanni, gleams in the torchlight, and the headstrong Albizzi and his fellow-rioters scatter like chaff before the onward rush of the paid soldiers of the house of Medici. Then, encompassed by a guard of bristling lances, liveried grooms, and torch-bearers, and followed by a crowd of shouting boys, masked revellers, and exultant retainers, the three lads hurried down the Via Larga; the great gates of the Palace of the Medici swung open to admit them, and the noise and riot of the carnival died away in the distance. Through the hall of arches and up the grand staircase the lads hastened to where, in the spacious *loggia*, or enclosed piazza, Lorenzo the Magnificent stood waiting to receive them.

"Well, well, my breathless young citizens," he exclaimed, "what news and noise of strife is this I hear? By San Marco, but you seem in such a sorry strait that I could almost say, with our excellent rhymester, good Ser Folgere:

"'How gallant are ye in your brave attires,
How bold ye look, true paladins of war, —
Stout-hearted are ye — as a hare in chase.'"

But his banter changed to solicitude as he noticed the troubled face of his son. "Who, then, is in fault, my Giovanni?" he asked. "'T was well for thee that Pietro sallied out in such hot haste; else, from all I hear, the Black Brothers of the Miserecordia might even now be bearing to Santa Maria, or the tomb, a prince of Holy Church, a son of the house of Medici, slain in a vile street brawl."

"Nay, hear, my father, I pray, the whole truth of the matter," Giovanni replied; and, as he relates, in presence of that brilliant and listening company, the story of the carnival fight as we already know it, let us, rather, read hastily the story of the great house of the Medici of Florence, whose princely head now stands before us — he whom the people call "*il gran magnifico*," Lorenzo the Magnificent, the father of the boy cardinal.

Four hundred years, and more, ago there lived in the beautiful Italian city of Firenze, or Florence, a wealthy family known as the Medici. They were what we now call capitalists — merchants and bankers, with ventures in many a land and with banking-houses in sixteen of the leading cities of Europe. Success in trade brought them wealth, and wealth brought them power, until, from simple citizens of a small inland republic they advanced to a position of influence and importance beyond that of many a king and prince of their day. At the time of our sketch, the head of the house was Lorenzo de Medici, called the Magnificent, from his wealth, his power, and his splendid and liberal hospitality. All Florence submitted to his will, and though the fair city was still, in form, a republic, the wishes and words of Lorenzo were as law to his fellow-citizens. A man of wonderful tact and of great attainments, he was popular with young and old, rich and poor.

From a glorious romp with the children, he would turn to a profound discussion with wise old philosophers or theologians, could devise means for loaning millions to the king of England, sack a city that had braved the power of Florence, or write the solemn hymns or gay street songs for the priests or for the people of his much loved city. Princes and poets, painters and priests, politicians and philosophers, sat at his bountiful table in the splendid palace at the foot of the Via Larga, or walked in his wonderful gardens of San Marco; rode "a-hawking" from his beautiful villa at Careggi, or joined in the wild frolic of his gorgeous street pageants. Power, such as his could procure or master any thing, and we therefore need not wonder that the two boys whose acquaintance we have made had been pushed into prominence to please the house of Medici. Look well at them again. The boy, who, with face upturned toward his father's kindly eyes, is telling the story of the street fight, is the second son of Lorenzo, Giovanni (or John) de Medici, Abbot of Passignano, and now, though scarcely fourteen, an unproclaimed cardinal of the Church of Rome — the future Leo X., the famous pope of Martin Luther's day. His companion is the young Giulio (or Julius) de Medici, nephew of Lorenzo, and already at thirteen Grand Prior of Capua and Knight of the Holy Order of St. John of Jerusalem. He, too, is to be in future years both cardinal and pope — that Clement VII., of whom you may read in history as the unfortunate prisoner of San Angelo, the antagonist of bluff King Henry VIII. of England. And this other lad, this Buonarotti, who is he? A protégé of Lorenzo, the companion of his sons and a favored guest at his table, his name is to last through the ages high above priest or prince or pope, more illustrious than all the Medici, the wonderful Michael-Angelo, the greatest of all the artists.

"So, so," Lorenzo said, as Giovanni concluded his story; "the matter is graver than I thought. 'T is another yelp from the Albizzi kennel. The Signory must look to it. Young Messer Francesco's tongue wags too freely for the city's good. But back to Pisa must ye go, my lads, for it ill beseems such as you, prelates and grave students of theology as ye are, to be ruffling with daggers drawn in any wild street-brawl that these troublous malcontents may raise against us."

And so back to the quiet University of Pisa went the boys Giovanni and Giulio to pursue their studies in "theology and ecclesiastical jurisprudence." Think how you feel, boys and girls, when, after a particularly jolly vacation, or an entrancing evening at the circus or the pantomime, you go back to what seem to you dull school studies, and then consider whether this boy cardinal, after all the glitter and parade and excitement of the carnival days, could be expected to fully relish his tasks of dry and laborious study. I imagine his solemn old biographer tells but half the truth when he writes: "The splendid exhibitions, the freedom and the songs with which the spectacles of Florence were accompanied, could scarcely have failed to banish at intervals that gravity of carriage which the young cardinal was directed to support"; — all of which is a very dry and roundabout way of saying that "boys will be boys," and that young Giovanni de Medici, cardinal though he was, loved mischief and excitement and frolic quite as much as have all healthy young fellows since the days of the very first boy.

Spending his time thus, between his stately Florentine home, his noble old castle of an abbey at Passignano, and the University of Pisa, Giovanni's three years of probation were passed. For a cardinal of thirteen was something out of the common even in those old days of intrigue and bribery, and Pope Innocent the Eighth, in making the appointment, had insisted that the ceremony of investment should not take place until Giovanni's sixteenth year.

"Whither so fast, my Maddalena?" asked young Francesco Albizzi, stopping a dark-haired flower-girl, as on a bright March morning he rode into the city. "What's astir, *cara mia*, that thou and all the world seem crowding to meet me, here, at San Gallo's gate?"

"Thou, indeed?" and the flower-girl laughed a merry peal. "Why, brother of the mole and lord of all the bats, where hast thou been asleep not to know that to-day our young Messer Giovanni is to be proclaimed a cardinal?"

"So — the little Medici again?" exclaimed the wrathful Albizzi. "May the *marzoccho* eat his heart! Must he be always setting the city upside down? Where is 't to be, Maddalena?"

"Why, where but at the altar of Fiesole? But do not thou keep me longer," she said, breaking away from the indignant young patriot. "All Florence goes forth to meet my lord cardinal at the Bridge of Mugnone, and my flowers will sell well and rarely to-day. But, hark thee, Messer Francesco," she added, with warning finger, "we are all *palleschi* [25] to-day, and 't were best for thee to swallow thy black words. See, yonder rides young Messer Pietro, and the Medici lances are ready and sharp for such as thou."

And, as Albizzi turned sullenly away, Maddalena disappeared in the crowd that, hurrying through San Gallo's gate, headed toward the flower-crowned hill of Fiesole. There, overlooking the "Beautiful City," stood the gray old monastery in which, on that eventful Sunday, the ninth of March, 1492, the young Giovanni received the vestments — the long scarlet frock, the mantle, cape, and train — that he was to wear as cardinal. With simple but solemn words, as one who had known from his very cradle this lad, now raised to so high a position and dignity, the worthy Fra Matteo Bosso, the Prior of Fiesole, conducted the rites of investiture, and the long-expected ceremony was accomplished.

"Illustrissimo," said Pietro de Medici, addressing his brother by the title which was now his right, "will it please your grace to return to our father's palace? All Florence waits to accompany thee from the Bridge of Mugnone."

So, into the city, attended by the Archbishop of Florence and the civil magistrates, with a glittering retinue, and followed by "an immense multitude on horseback and on foot," with waving banners and shouts of joyous welcome, through the great gate of San Gallo, rode Giovanni de Medici, "on a barded mule housed with trappings of scarlet and gold," to where, in the arched hall of the palace of the Medici, his father, sick and reclining on his litter, awaited the coming of the boy cardinal.

"You are not only the youngest of the cardinals, my Giovanni, but the youngest ever raised to that rank," Lorenzo said, after his warm congratulations had been given. "Endeavor, then, to alleviate the burthen of your early dignity by the regularity of your life and by your perseverance in those studies which are suitable to your profession. Be vigilant, be unassuming, be cautious, and deliberate every evening on what you may have to perform the following day, that you may not be unprepared for whatever may happen."

With these and other words of useful and practical advice did the proud father counsel the young cardinal, and then, from all the acclamations and illuminations, the joy, the fireworks, and the feasting that accompanied the ceremonies at Florence, Giovanni, on the twelfth of March, with a brilliant retinue, departed for Rome. Here, on the fifteenth of March, the Pope, with much pomp, received him "in full consistory," as it is called, welcomed him as a new member of the "College of Cardinals," and gave him the "holy kiss." Placing the great scarlet hat on the boy's head as he knelt before him, the Pope next encircled his finger with the sapphire ring — emblem of fidelity and loyalty, — and the boy arose, by the appointment and creation of Pope Innocent VIII., "the Most Illustrious and Most Reverend Lord Cardinal Giovanni de Medici."

Thus far we have seen only the bright side of the picture — the carnival glories, the processions, the ceremonies, the cheers, the frolic, the feasting. Now comes the darker side; for if ever a boy was to be in trouble, worried, badgered, and disappointed, that boy was "the Most Illustrious and Most Reverend Lord Cardinal Giovanni de Medici." For, like a sudden shock, with many an accompanying "portent" and "sign" that caused the superstitious Florentines to shake their heads in dismay, came the news that Lorenzo the Magnificent was dead. Still in the prime of life, with wealth and power and a host of followers, a mysterious disease laid hold upon him, and on the eighth of April, 1492, he died at his beautiful villa among the olive groves of Careggi, where the windows overlooked the fair valley of the Arno and the "Beautiful Florence" that he had ruled so long. From Rome to Florence, and from Florence to Rome again, the young cardinal posted in anxious haste, as following fast upon the death of his much-loved father came the sudden illness and death of his other patron and protector, Pope Innocent VIII. This occurred on July 25, 1492, and soon again was Giovanni posting back to Florence, a fugitive from Rome, proscribed by the new Pope, Alexander VI., the bitter and relentless enemy of the house of Medici.

But, in Florence, Lorenzo the Magnificent was dead, and in his place ruled his eldest son, Messer Pietro. Rash, headstrong, overbearing, vindictive, wavering, proud, and imprudent, this wayward young man of twenty-one succeeded to a power he could not wield and to possessions he could not control. Enemies sprung up, old friends and supporters dropped away, the people lost confidence, and when, by a final blunder, he unnecessarily surrendered to the king of France important Florentine fortresses and territory, the anger of his fellow-citizens broke out in fierce denunciation and open revolt.

There is no merry shouting of titles, no gay carnival dress, no glittering pageant now, as, on the morning of Sunday, the ninth of November, 1494, the young cardinal and his cousin Giulio pass anxiously down the grand staircase of the Medici palace to where in the great entrance-hall the pikestaffs and arquebuses of the Swiss guard ring on the marble floor.

"Think you the Signory will admit him?" Giulio asked of his cousin, as they awaited the return of Pietro from his demand for admittance to the palace of the Signory, the city hall of Florence.

"'T is a question for an older head than mine, Giulio," replied Giovanni. "Pietro's hot-headedness and the Signory's unreasonable demands may cause a conflict, and the people, I fear me, are so excitable that — — but hark! what was that?" he asked hastily as there fell upon their ears the long *boom* — *boom* — of a tolling bell.

"By San Marco, the people are up!" said Giulio, excitedly. "'T is the *campana*; 't is the mad bellow of the old cow of the Vacca! Quick, stand to your arms, Giovanni, for soon all Florence will be at your doors!"

Too well the boys knew the meaning of that tolling bell —

the great bell of the Palazzo Vecchio, "the old cow of the Vacca," as the Florentines called it. Its loud *boom — boom —* meant "Danger for Florence!" And, as its clang sounded over the city from gate to gate, every citizen, no matter what he might be doing, answered the summons by snatching up the arms that were handiest and hastening to the great square of the Vecchio.

"Pietro is lost!" shouted the cardinal. "*Palle, palle!* Medici to the rescue!" But, before the guard could rally to his summons, the door burst open, and in rushed Pietro de Medici, called the Lord of Florence, white-faced and bespattered with mud, while at his heels followed a dozen equally terrified men-at-arms. Without, the yells and hootings of an angry mob filled the air, and the deeper cry of "Liberty, liberty for the people!" sounded above the din.

"Well, my brother?" was all the cardinal said.

Messer Pietro caught him by the arm. "Quick, send for Orsini and his troops!" he cried excitedly. "Send now, or all is lost, Giovanni. The people are up! The Signory refuses me — me, the Lord of Florence — admittance to the palace. Magistrates whom our father honored and appointed reviled and insulted me; men and women who have lived on our bounty, nay, even the very children hooted and pelted me as I turned from the wicket of the Signory, and now, by the claws of the *marzoccho*! I will have in Orsini's troops and drench the streets with blood."

"Hold, hold, Pietro; not so fast, I pray," Giovanni exclaimed. "Is there no loyalty, no respect for the Medici left in Florence?. To horse, and follow me! It shall not be said that the sons of Lorenzo the Magnificent lost their lordship without a struggle."

Again the palace gates were swung open; again the lily-banner of Florence and the ball-escutcheon of the Medici flashed through the city streets as, followed by Giulio and the Swiss halberdiers, the boy cardinal rode toward the palace of the Signory.

"*Palle, palle!* Medici! ho, Medici!" rang the well-known cry of the great house as the armed guard of the cardinal pressed through the crowded streets.

"Hollo, my Lord Cardinal; well met again!" shouted a mocking voice, and around from the great square of the Duomo came Francesco Albizzi and a motley crowd of followers.

"Back, Albizzi, back!" Giovanni commanded. "Our business is with the Signory and not with feud-breeders such as art thou."

"Ho, hark to the little Illustrissimo! *Popolo! ho, popolo!*" Albizzi shouted, and the surging and excited mass swarmed around Giovanni's little band with the ringing cry: "*Popolo, popolo! Liberta, liberta!*" (The people, the people! Liberty for the people.)

All the stout bravery of the lad flashed into his olive cheeks, and the power that belonged to his title of cardinal gave him strength and nerve.

"Men of Florence," he cried, as he rose in his stirrups, "have ye no memories of past benefits received from the house of Medici, ever the helpers of the people? Have ye no memories of the good Lorenzo, the brother of the citizens of Florence? Have ye no reverence for the Church whose instrument I am? Francesco Albizzi, traitor to Florence and the Church, — back, back, on thy life, or I, — even I, — the Cardinal de Medici, will cast upon thy head the curse of Holy Church!"

The crowd wavered and fell back before the determined stand of the young prelate, and even Albizzi's head bent under the priestly threat. But, just then, there sounded again on the air the sullen *boom* — *boom* — of the *campana*, and the cry, "*Popolo, popolo!*" rose again from the mob.

"Fly, fly, my Lord Cardinal," said a quick voice, and, turning, Giovanni saw a masked figure and felt a touch upon his bridle-arm. "'T is I, Buonarotti," said the new-comer, slightly raising his visor. "The Signory have declared both thee and Pietro rebels and outlaws! A price is set upon thy head. Pietro has fled already, and when once the news is known, not even thy cardinal's robes nor thy noble name can save thee from the mob."

Giovanni looked at the rapidly increasing crowd, looked at his insufficient guard, already deserting him in fear, and then said, sadly:

"'T were better to die for our house than to desert it, but how will it avail? Come, Giulio," — and, slipping from their horses, the two lads, guided by Buonarotti and a few faithful friends, escaped from the yelling mob into a small tavern, where disguises were in readiness. The cardinal's scarlet robes and the knight's crossleted tunic were exchanged for the gray habits of Franciscan monks, and then, in sorrow and dismay, the boy cardinal fled from his native city. As he hurried through San Gallo's massive gate, with the *boom* — *boom*, of that terrible bell still tolling the doom of his family, and the "*Popolo; liberta!*" of an aroused and determined people filling the air, he remembered the brilliance and enthusiasm of other passages through that well-known gate, and with the words "Ungrateful, — ah, ungrateful," on his lips, he hastened to the villa at beautiful Careggi, where the defeated Pietro had taken temporary refuge.

But not long could the banished brothers remain at Careggi. "Two thousand crowns of gold to him who will bring to the Signory at Florence the head of either of the outlawed Medici; five thousand crowns to him who will deliver to the Signory the bodies of these pestilent rebels alive." Thus read the cruel ban of their native city and, first, Pietro, and next, Giovanni, turned from the familiar scenes of their loved country-house and fled in great secrecy toward Bologna. But the hunters were after them, and for two anxious weeks this young Giovanni, a cardinal of Rome and a prince of Holy Church, whose boyish days had been filled with pleasure and brightness, whose slightest wish had ever been gratified, remained concealed, in the deepest recesses of the Apennines, a rebel and an outlaw, with a price upon his head.

Eighteen years passed away, and on the morning of the fourteenth of September, 1512, two full-robed priests, surrounded by a great escort of glittering lances and a retinue of heavy-armed foot-soldiers, entered the gate-way of the "Beautiful City." They were the Cardinal de Medici and his faithful cousin returning to their native city, proudly and triumphantly, after eighteen years of exile. Boys no longer, but grave and stalwart men, Giovanni and Giulio rode through the familiar streets and past the old landmarks that they had never forgotten, to where, at the foot of the Via Larga, still stood the palace of the Medici. Since the year 1504, when the unfortunate Messer Pietro — unfortunate to the last — had been drowned on the disastrous retreat from Garigliano, the Cardinal Giovanni had stood as the head of the house of Medici. High in favor with the stern old Pope Julius II., he had, after six years of wandering and anxiety, risen to eminence and power at Rome. In all these eighteen years, he never gave up his hope of regaining his native city. Three times did the Medici seek to return to power; three times were they repulsed. At last, his time has come. Florence, torn by feud and discontent, with a Spanish army camped beyond her walls, opens her gates to the conquerors, and the Cardinal Giovanni rules as Lord of Florence.

So the fair city again lost her liberties; so the exiled family returned to position and power; so the fickle Florentines, who, in a fury of patriotism, had sacked the palace of Lorenzo, now shouted themselves hoarse for "*Palle* and the Medici!"

And within less than six months comes a still higher triumph. Pope Julius II. is dead, and, by the unanimous voice of the "College of Cardinals," Giovanni, Cardinal de Medici, ascends the papal throne, on the third of March, 1513, as Pope Leo the Tenth.

With his later life, we need not here concern ourselves. The story of the boy may perhaps lead you to read in history the interesting story of the man. Only thirty-seven, the youngest of the popes, as he was the youngest of the cardinals, he wore the triple tiara in the stormy days of the great Reformation, and made his court the centre of learning and refinement, so that his reign has been called "the golden age of Italian art and letters." He is well worth remembrance also as having been the firm friend of the American Indians amid the cruel persecutions of their Spanish conquerors. "The best of all the Medici, save his father," and "the only pope who has bestowed his own name upon his age," — so the historians report, — we may, as we read of him, remember the boyishness, notwithstanding his high position, the diligence, notwithstanding his love of pleasure, and the loyalty to the name and fortunes of a once powerful family, that marked the youthful years of Giovanni de Medici, the Boy Cardinal.

FOOTNOTES:

[22] The *marzoccho* was the great stone lion of the Palazzo Vecchio.

[23] The *Palle d' Oro*, or golden balls, were the arms of the house of Medici, and "*Palle, palle!*" was their rallying cry.

[24] The Church of the Reparata, or Santa Maria Novella, in which Lorenzo the Magnificent was wounded and his brother Giuliano murdered, in the conspiracy of the Pazzi, in 1478.

[25] *Palleschi* was the name given to the adherents and retainers of the house of Medici.

IX. IXTLIL' OF TEZCUCO — THE BOY CACIQUE.

(Afterward King of Tezcuco, the last of the ruling Aztec princes.)
A.D. 1515.

A dusky courier, fleet-footed and wary-eyed, dashed swiftly along the roadway that, three spear-lengths wide, spanned the green plain and led from the royal city to the Palace of the Hill, the wonderful rural retreat of the good 'Hualpilli, the 'tzin [26] or lord of Tezcuco. Through the sculptured gate-way he sped, past the terraced gardens and the five hundred porphyry steps, past the three reservoirs of the Marble Women, past the Winged Lion and the Rock of the Great 'Tzin to where, in the midst of a grove of giant cedars, rose the fairy-like walls of the beautiful summer palace of the king.

"At the baths," said a watchful guardsman, upon whose quilted suit of cotton mail and on whose wooden wolf's-head helmet glistened the feather badge of the 'tzin. Scarcely slackening his speed the courier turned from the palace door-way and plunged into the thick shadows of the cypress forest. He followed the course of the foaming cascade which came rushing and tumbling over the rocks through a mass of flowers and odorous shrubs, and stopped suddenly before the marble portico of an airy pavilion, where a flight of steps cut in the solid porphyry and polished like mirrors, led down to the baths of the 'tzin. For an instant the courier stood erect and motionless as a statue, then, swiftly stooping to the earth, he laid the open palm of his right hand on the ground and next raised it slowly to his head, offering with downcast eyes the scroll he had carried in the folds of his maxtlatl [27] to the inmate of the marble pavilion — 'Hualpilli the Just, the 'tzin of Tezcuco.

"From the Council?" asked the 'tzin, as he took the scroll.

"From the Council, O King," replied the courier, falling prostrate on the ground as he heard the voice of his lord.

The face of the 'tzin wore a perplexed and troubled expression as he unrolled the scroll. "Again?" he said; "Is the boy at his tricks again? How shall hot young blood be tamed for soberer duties?"

And what is it on the soft and polished surface of the maguey [28] paper that so disturbs the worthy 'tzin? It seems a series of comic pictures painted in vivid green and red. First, a blazing sun; then a boy with a big head and a boy with a small head topped with two flags; then a misshapen-looking man with a short cloak and a long staff and above his head a plume; then a low-roofed house, a footprint under a blazing sun; and, lastly, a man sitting on the ground. What do you make of all this, as, especially privileged, you peep over the shoulder of 'Hualpilli the 'tzin, in the portico of his porphyry baths? Nothing, of course. But to the dusky king, skilled in the reading of Aztec hieroglyphics, the message from his Council is plain enough. And this is what he reads: "Most dread and mighty lord, the sun of the world! This is to inform you that the noble young cacique, Ixtlil', at the head of forty of his wild boy-followers is raiding the streets of Tezcuco, and has already assaulted and wofully distressed full four hundred of the townspeople. Hasten, then, we pray you, your royal feet, that you may see and believe our statement, lest if we may not stop the noble young cacique in this his dangerous sport, your royal city of Tezcuco shall be disturbed and overturned as if by an earthquake."

"Runs he so rudely?" said the 'tzin. "I will even see this for myself. So much of fighting mettle in a little lad must not waste itself upon those whom he may one day rule," and borne by his slaves to the villa he ordered that his litter be made ready at once. It soon awaited him, gleaming with gold and bright with green plumes. Turning with a sigh from the calm retreat he loved so much, he ascended his litter and commanded: "To the city, straight," and the trained litter-bearers were soon speeding across the green plain, bearing their lord to his royal city of Tezcuco, two leagues distant, near the shores of the great salt lake. But, ere he reached the city walls, he descended from his litter, dismissed his slaves, and, drawing over his kingly dress a *tilmatli*, or long purple cloak of fine cotton, he mingled with the crowd that surged through the city gate.

Meanwhile, on one of the wide and smoothly cemented

streets that traversed the beautiful city of Tezcuco there was great commotion and excitement. For at the head of his amateur train-band of forty Aztec boys, Ixtlil', the young cacique, [29] or prince, of Tezcuco, was charging in mimic fight, past palace gate-ways and low *adobe* walls, across the great square of the *tinguez*, or market-place, and over the bridges that spanned the main canal, scattering group after group of unarmed and terrified townspeople like sheep before his boyish spears, while the older warriors laughed loud at the dangerous sport, and the staid old "uncles" or councillors of the king dared not interfere with the pranks and pleasures of this wild and unruly young son of the 'tzin, their lord and master.

Near the serpent-sculptured wall of the great *teocalli*, or temple to 'Huitzil the Aztec god of war, a number of citizens, unwilling to be longer badgered and persecuted by a boy, cacique though he was, had gathered to make a stand against the rough play of the turbulent lads! Round from the great market-place, with the shrill Aztec whistle that, years after, the Spanish invaders learned to know so well, swung the corps of youthful marauders, their uniform a complete mimicry of the brave Tezcucan warriors. Gay cotton doublets, surcoats of feather-mail, bristling wolf-crests dyed with cochineal, plumes and lances, banners and devices, gleamed in the clear Mexican sunlight, and, leading all this riot, came a boy of scarce fourteen, whose *panache*, or head-dress, of bright green feathers denoted his royal birth as it drooped over the long black hair that covered a face of pale bronze. In his hand, he brandished a broad *maquahuitl*, or sharp Aztec sword made of the polished *itzli* stone.

"Ho, yield ye, yield ye, slaves!" he cried; "tribute or bodies to the lords of the streets!"

"Tribute, tribute or bodies to the young cacique!" shouted his boy-followers. "Way there; way for the grandson of the Hungry-Fox!" [30]

Their rush was irresistible, and the terrified townsfolk, repenting of their determination to stand in their own defence, when once they had caught the gleam of the *maquahuitl*, and faced the fierce presence of the boy cacique, turned to hurried flight beneath the walls of the great *teocalli*.

"What, are ye all cowards to flee from a pack of boys! Women and daughters of women are ye, and not men of proud Tezcuco!"

The taunt came from a tall and well-built man who strode into the midst of the rout. His *tilmatli*, or cotton cloak completely enveloped his figure, while the long staff in his hand showed him to be a traveller, a visitor probably from Tenochtitlan or distant Cholula. "Back, boys, back," he commanded, "back, I tell you and let me pass!"

The shrill war-whistle of young Ixtlil' rang out loud and clear, and his fierce young troop with a startling war-cry clattered round the daring stranger.

"Now by the fire plumes of Quetzal'!" [31] cried the headstrong young prince, "who be ye to brave the son of the king? To me, comrades all, and down with the stranger!"

The be-cloaked unknown backed against the stout walls of the *teocalli*. With an easy turn of his staff he parried the vicious sword thrust of the boy cacique and sent his polished *maquahuitl* spinning through the air. Then with a swinging sweep he laid lustily about him, right and left, scattering the throng of boy soldiers until a good dozen or so lay on the cemented roadway or with aching heads scud out of range of that terrible staff. With a sudden dash the stranger grasped the young cacique's feather-cloak, and catching him by the nape of the neck shook him so roundly that the green *panache* tumbled from the lad's head and his princely teeth chattered with the shock.

The timid citizens, reassured by this signal discomfiture of their boy-pests, had drawn to the aid of the stranger, but they trembled at this rough handling of the young prince, and the lad's boy-followers, still at a respectful distance from the stranger's staff, cried loudly: "Ho, rescue, rescue for Ixtlil' the cacique! Death, death to the sacrilegious slave who dares lay hand upon the son of the 'tzin!"

The wolf-casques of the king's spearmen came pouring from the market-place, pressing close behind the royal banner of Tezcuco, the golden coyatl, or winged fox. A hundred copper lance-heads, aimed for flight, pointed at the bold stranger's heart. But all unmoved he raised his staff. "He who lays hands upon the favored of the gods," he said, "must needs know when and why he does so"; then casting off the purple *tilmatli* and drooping hood, that had disguised him, "Now, who shall say me nay?" he asked, and valiant spearmen, timid citizens, and bold boy-soldiers, with a startled cry of surprise, went down in the dust in abject homage before their lord and master, 'Hualpilli the Just, the 'tzin of Tezcuco. [32]

Haulpilli The Lord Of Tezcuco Reveals Himself, — *"Now Who Shall Say Me Nay?" He Asked.*

With a loud whistle the 'tzin summoned the slaves who bore his litter. They came hurrying to his call, and soon, followed by the youthful and somewhat sobered band of boy-soldiers, wondering townsfolk, and a mass of royal spearmen, the wild young cacique accompanied his father to the great palace of the kings of Tezcuco.

Upon the map of modern Mexico you can readily find Tezcuco, now an insignificant manufacturing town, some sixteen miles north-east of the city of Mexico, near the shores of the salt lake of Tezcuco. Its *adobe* or mud houses shelter scarce five thousand squalid inhabitants, and of the former grandeur of the "Imperial City" of the old Aztec days there remains, as one traveller remarks, "not a wreck — not even an epitaph."

But, according to the historians of that wonderful achievement of four centuries back — the Conquest of Mexico — Tezcuco, "City of Rest," was, in the year of our story, 1515, the mighty capital of one of the most fertile and lovely sections of the old Aztec land of Anahuac, a city of over one hundred and fifty thousand inhabitants, and second only in population, power, and magnificence to the royal "City of the Cactus and the Rock" — Tenochtitlan, known ever to Europeans as the City of Mexico. Temples and palaces, schools and gardens, aqueducts, causeways, streets, and walls adorned and defended the beautiful "City of Rest," and so great was its culture and refinement that, as Tenochtitlan, or Mexico, was called the Venice, so Tezcuco "claimed the glory of being the Athens of the New World."

In one of the long and richly decorated arcades which led from the king's apartments to the baths and gardens of the low-walled but far-reaching palace of Tezcuco, two boys with their scorers were playing at *totoloque* the day after young Ixtlil's street combat. Now *totoloque* was the favorite ball-game of the Aztecs, young and old. It consisted simply of pitching balls, made of some hard and polished substance, at a mark, at long or short distances, according to the expertness of the players, the first complete score of five throws to take the prize. The game was frequently close and exciting, as was the case in this particular game in the arcades of the palace. And the brown-skinned little Tula was scoring for the cacique Ixtlil', while the young prince Cacama scored for the cacique Tecocal', the opponent of Ixtlil'. Now the prince Cacama was the eldest son of the 'tzin 'Hualpilli, and, as older brothers often will — modern ones as well as ancient — he liked to assert his authority and superiority over his younger brothers and half-brothers. For that great palace in old Tezcuco held a large family of boys and girls.

"There, Teco," the cacique Ixtlil' cried triumphantly, as the golden ball struck fair and square against the golden target; "there's my fifth throw and the game is mine again. Oh, there is no use in your trying to pitch against the champion. So, pass over the golden quills, Cacama!" [33]

"That will I not," exclaimed the prince Cacama. "We know enough not to trust to your scoring, and I've kept tally too. Show me the maguey, Tula."

The little girl handed the parchment to her brother. "I thought so; I thought so," he cried. "See here, Teco, she's scored one for the time when his ball plumped into the fish-fountain, and one for the shot that knocked over my cup of chocolate! what do you say to that!"

"*Ixoxal; ixoxal!*" [34] exclaimed the young Teco; "then it's not fair and the game is ours, Cacama!"

"But, Cacama," pleaded little Tula in her own behalf, "It wasn't my fault; I only put down what Ixtlil' told me to."

"Ho, Tula," cried young Teco, contemptuously; "haven't you played *totoloque* enough with Ixtlil' to know how nimble he is with his score. Why, he could fool Maxtla the juggler with his eyes open. Don't give him the gold quills, Cacama. He didn't win them."

"I say I did," shouted the angry Ixtlil', snatching at the gleaming quills. "Give me the gold quills, Cacama, or I'll order up my boys and force them from you."

"Oh! will you though!" Cacama said, mockingly; "well, my valorous young captain, take my advice and don't be quite so ready with your young ruffians. Our father's councillors have reminded him of the star-men's prophecy since your frolic of yesterday, and have advised him to do what the wise men suggested when they cast your horoscope."

"And what was that?" asked the young cacique carelessly, as he tossed the golden balls in air and caught them dexterously.

"Why, to take your life at once," replied the prince Cacama; "lest when you grow to manhood you overturn the throne of your fathers and give up Tezcuco to the strangers and to blood."

"What!" exclaimed the boy, turning quickly upon his elder brother, "the old dotards dared advise my father to take my life? And you, you, my very loving brother, stood by and let them live after such rebel words?"

"And why should I not?" coolly answered Cacama. "The boy who can pitch his poor nurse into a well because she doesn't please his little lordship will not hesitate to throw a nation into strife if so the fancy takes him. The boy who tries his hand at *ixoxal* in *totoloque* will not stop at darker work when the prize is a throne. If the king our father were not such a believer in fate and in this fable of the return of the white god to Anahuac, my word for it you would ere this have been sacrificed to "Huitzil' as the old 'uncles' did advise."

"Cacama," burst out the young Ixtlil' now hot with bitter passion, "you are a coward *tamane*! [35] and, as for those open-mouthed councillors who would have my father take my life from me — from me, the Cacique Ixtlil' — from me, the boy captain — by the white robes of Haloc! [36] I'll make them rue their words ere yet this day's sun cross the dome of the Smoking Hill! [37] If I am to overturn the throne of my fathers as the lying star-men prophesied, then shall not these same babbling 'uncles' live to see the day!" And ere his brother could stop him the enraged boy flung the golden *totoloque* balls into the sparkling fish-fountain, dashed through the curling clouds of incense that wreathed the wide door-way of the sculptured arcade, and breathing out threatening and slaughter against the offending gray-beards, hurried from his father's palace.

Once again terror and commotion filled the streets of Tezcuco, as, at the head of his boyish band, Ixtlil' the young cacique, bent on instant revenge, stormed the houses of the old lords of his father's council and, one after another, dragged them from their homes. The people, thronging the *azoteas*, or broad, flat roofs of the low-walled houses, looked down in wonder and dismay upon this strangest of sights — six gray and honorable "uncles" or councillors of the king, bound neck to neck by the "manacles," or poles with leathern yokes, and driven through the city streets by a band of forty boys.

Young Ixtlil's vengeance was sharp and sudden. Ere night fell upon the city the dreadful garrote — the strangling stick and cord — plied by the boy executioners had done its dreadful work, and the six offending councillors lay dead in the *tinguez*, by the order of the fierce boy whom they had offended. And only when the last gray head had fallen a victim to boyish wrath did the stupor of surprise that had held the people give place to action. Then the bowmen of the king swept down upon the boy's brigade, and overcoming all resistance, took the young leader captive and dragged him for speedy sentence before his father, 'Hualpilli the 'tzin.

"I'll Make Them Rue Their Words Ere This Day's Sun Cross The Dome Of The Smoking Hill."

Ixtlil' the cacique knew what to expect. He could hope for no mercy from the king, who was called by his subjects the Wise and Just. He had committed an offence against the state that was punishable with death, and he remembered how, years before, this same wise and just king, his father, had condemned his eldest son to death for breaking the laws of the realm. But with the same Indian stoicism that marked the Aztec, as it did the less cultivated

Algonquin and Sioux, the boy went, unresistingly, to meet his fate.

The 'tzin 'Hualpilli sat upon the "King's Tribunal" in his great hall of judgment. A gorgeous feather canopy emblazoned with the royal arms of the lords of Tezcuco hung above his head, and, seated thus, he gave audience to subjects and embassies, and sent out his fleet runners with royal dispatches to his governors and vassal rulers. Turning his head as he heard in the outer court a sudden and great commotion, his face grew troubled and anxious as he saw the cause of the tumult to be his favorite son, Ixtlil', bound, and in the hands of his officers of justice. For, spite of the lad's wild ways, the good 'tzin loved this unruly young cacique, and saw in his excesses and troublesome pranks the promise of a courage that might make him, in the years to come, a stalwart soldier and defender of the throne of his fathers. But justice must take its course and 'Hualpilli the 'tzin was called the Wise and Just.

"What charge bring you against this lad?" he asked, as captive and captors prostrated themselves before the "King's Tribunal." And when he had heard the details of the terrible crime of the young cacique he simply demanded of his son, "Are these things so?" and the boy boldly answered, "Yes, my Lord the King."

Then the face of the 'tzin grew stern and sombre. Rising, he said: "This is now no prank of an idle boy. It is a crime against the state and against the gods who rule the state. Lead him to the 'Tribunal of the Gods,'" and, attended by fourteen of his lords of highest rank, the king walked solemnly to where, across the great judgment-hall, another throne, called "the Tribunal of the Gods," faced "the King's Tribunal." It was the seat from which sentence of death was pronounced, and was a marvellous creation. Above a throne of pure gold was suspended a great feather canopy of many and brilliant hues, from the centre of which gleamed a blazing sun, made all of gold and jewels. Rich hangings of rare and colored fans, looped up with rings of gold and embroidered with many strange devices, lined the walls of the alcove which held the awful throne. Before the throne, high on a heap of weapons of war, shields and quivers and bows and arrows, rested a human skull, circled by an emerald crown and topped with a crest of feathered plumes and jewels.

Placing the triple crown of Tezcuco upon his head and taking in his hand the golden arrow of judgment, the 'tzin said to his son: "Ixtlil-o-chitl, cacique of Tezcuco, I charge you in the presence of the arrow and the skull to say, if you can, why sentence of death should not now be spoken against you for this, your wicked deed."

And the boy cacique, first prostrating himself before "the Tribunal of the Gods," rose and said: "O most dread Lord, my father and my king, I have in this matter done no more than is my right as a cacique of Tezcuco and as your son. For you have ever told me that to prepare for the life of a soldier is the best and noblest work befitting a son of Tezcuco and of Anahuac. You have said that this ambition was the only one worthy a cacique who, as I am, is the son and grandson of mighty kings. You have told me that a soldier is justified in defending his life, for that his life belongs to the state, and, more than this, that the life of a royal prince is doubly the state's. These your councillors, whom I have justly punished, have sought to turn your affection from me, your son, and only because I wished to prepare for a soldier's life, and to train my band of boys to deeds of daring and to love of war. They sought to take away my life, and I have acted but as you, my king and father, did counsel me. If they have suffered death, then have they only obtained what they had intended for me. I struck before they could seize the chance to strike at me — even as in *totoloque*, O King most Just and Wise, the game was rightly mine, because my score was reached the quickest and my aim was surest."

And the old Tezcucan chronicler says that "the king found much force in these reasons." Removing his crown from his head and dropping the arrow of judgment from his hand, he stepped down from "the Tribunal of the Gods," and, taking his son's hand, said: "Hear, people of Tezcuco! I cannot, in justice or in right, sentence this lad for what was not malice, but simply the overflow of a boy's daring spirit — a spirit that may in after years do great deeds in your defence and for the state's security," and so with a lecture and a stern warning "not to do so again," the boy culprit was set free — an unjust and far too lenient judgment it seems to us at this distance for so foul a deed.

Years passed away. The words of the good 'tzin proved true enough, as the boy cacique grew to be so dashing and daring a warrior that, before the age of seventeen, he had won for himself the rank and insignia of a valorous and trusted captain in the armies of Tezcuco. Still the years passed, and now 'Hualpilli the 'tzin, the Wise and Just, was dead. Amid great pomp and the sacrifice of three hundred slaves his body was cremated on a funeral pile, rich in jewels and incense and precious stuffs, and his royal dust, sealed in a golden urn, was placed in the great *teocalli*, or temple of 'Huitzil. His sons, Cacama and Ixtlil' both claimed the throne of Tezcuco, and as in duty bound laid the question for settlement before Montezuma, the lord and sovereign of all Anahuac. The Mexican emperor decided in favor of the elder brother, and hot with rage and wrath the defeated Ixtlil' withdrew to his little mountain princedom among the Cordilleras, biding his time for revenge. For the vindictive spirit of the boy, you see, never disciplined, increased with his years. The day for revenge arrived all too soon, for in the year 1519 came the Conquest. The Spaniards, first hailed as gods by the Aztecs, because of their fair skins, their "canoes with wings," their armor, their horses, and their artillery, conquered the country, laid waste the fair cities of the lakes and the valley, and, with iron heel, stamped out the last vestiges of Aztec civilization — "a civilization that," as one historian says, "might have instructed Europe."

And foremost in this work of destruction and of death stood Ixtlilochitl of Tezcuco, a traitor to his home-land, the vassal and the ally of Cortez the Spaniard. The prophecies of the "star-men" and the warnings of his father's councillors were fulfilled. He "united with the enemies of his country and helped to overturn its institutions and its religion."

Raised to the vacant throne of his father by the sword of Cortez ere yet he was twenty years old, Ixtlil' the cacique reigned for years as the last king of Tezcuco, and, converted to Christianity, was baptized under the Spanish name of Don Fernando, by which he was ever afterward known. Through all the dreadful days of Spanish conquest and Aztec patriotism he remained the firm friend and ally of the conquerors of his native land. For nearly a hundred years, in the grimy little chapel of St. Francis in the city of Tezcuco, the bones of these two friends lay side by side — Spaniard and Aztec, Cortez the conqueror and Ixtlil' the vassal, the once fierce and vindictive boy cacique of Tezcuco, who, wayward and hot-tempered as a lad, became the recreant as a man. Out of his hatred for Montezuma and for the brother who had supplanted him, Ixtlil', the last of the Aztec princes, turned his sword against the brave and beautiful land that had given him birth, thus achieving, says Prescott, the brilliant historian of the conquest, "the melancholy glory of having contributed more than any other chieftain of Anahuac to rivet the chains of the white man round the necks of his countrymen."

FOOTNOTES:

[26] 'Tzin is the Aztec for prince, or lord. Thus the last of the Montezumas, the noblest of Aztec heroes, was Guatemo-tzin, the 'tzin or prince Guatemo.

[27] Maxtlatl, the girdle or wide sash worn by runners and soldiers in battle.

[28] Maguey, the great Mexican aloe, from the leaves of which the Aztec made their paper. This wonderful plant indeed was, as Prescott says, "meat, drink, clothing and writing materials to the Aztecs."

[29] "Cacique in Mexico and prince in Wales." — Byron.

[30] "The Hungry Fox" (Nezahual-Cayotl), "the greatest monarch who ever sat upon an Indian throne," according to Prescott the historian, was the father of Nezahual-pilli, the 'tzin of Tezcuco and the grandfather of Ixtlilochitl the boy cacique. The story of his life is full of marvel, and he was altogether one of the most attractive and remarkable characters in Aztec history.

[31] Quetzal-Coatl, the Aztec god of the air. He was said to be fair-skinned, and the Aztecs had a prophecy that promised his return to earth. Hence the Spanish invaders were, at first, taken for gods and but little resistance offered them. Read General Lew Wallace's beautiful Aztec story: "The Fair God."

[32] The kings of Tezcuco, like that celebrated Caliph of Arabian story, Haroun al-Raschid, would often mix in disguise with their people, talking with all classes, and frequently rewarding merit and punishing wrong-doers.

[33] Transparent quills filled with gold dust, bags of cacao, (shining chocolate beans), and bits of tin cut in the form of a T, made up the circulating currency, or money, of the Aztecs.

[34] *Ixoxal*, an Aztec word applied to cheating in the game of *totoloque*, and signifying false scoring.

[35] *Tamane*, the lowest order of Aztec slaves. Used as a term of contempt among the higher classes.

[36] Haloc, the Aztec god of the sea.

[37] "The Smoking Hill," the signification of the name of the great Mexican volcano, Popocatepetl.

X. LOUIS OF BOURBON, THE BOY KING.

(Louis XIV. of France; afterward known as the Grand Monarque.)
A.D. 1651.

"Hush!" Pretty little Olympia Mancini's night-capped head bobbed inquiringly out of the door that opened into the corridor of the Gallery of Illustrious Personages in the old Palais Royal, as a long, low, distant murmur fell upon her ears.

"Hark!" Through the opposite door popped the sleep-tousled head of the awakened Armand, the bright young Count of Guiche, as hoarser and higher rose the angry sound, while, in the Queen's Gallery, stout old Guitat, captain of the regent's guard, stopped in his rounds to listen. Louder and nearer it came until it startled even the queen regent herself. Then the quick, sharp roll of the *rataplan* sounded through the miserable streets of the old city, as with ever-increasing shouts of "*Aux armes! aux armes!* They are stealing the king!" all Paris swarmed down the Rue de Honoré, and clamored at the outer gates of the great Palais Royal.

Did you ever hear or see a mob, boys and girls? Probably not; but ask father, or mother, or uncle, or any one you know who has ever had such an experience, if he thinks there is any sound more terrifying than that threatening, far-away murmur that grows each second louder and more distinct, until it swells and surges up and down the city streets — the hoarse, mad shouts of a mob. It was such a sound as this that on that dreary midnight of the tenth of February, 1651, filled the dark and narrow and dismal streets of old Paris, startling all the inmates of the Palais Royal, as under the palace windows rose the angry cry:

"The King! the King! Down with Mazarin!" The two anxious-faced young persons, a girl and a boy of thirteen or thereabout, who were peeping out into the corridor, looked at one another inquiringly.

"Whatever is the matter, Count?" asked dainty little Olympia, the pretty niece of the Queen's prime-minister, Mazarin.

But for answer the light-hearted young Armand, Count of

Guiche, whom even danger could not rob of gaiety, whistled softly the air that all rebellious Paris knew so well:

"A wind of the Fronde
Has this evening set in;
I think that it blows
'Gainst Monsieur Mazarin.
A wind of the Fronde
Has this evening set in!"

"The Fronde!" exclaimed Olympia, hastily; "why, what new trick do they play?"

"Faith, mam'selle," the boy count replied, "'t is a trick that may set us all a livelier dance than your delightful *la bransle*. The people are storming the palace to save the little king from your noble uncle, my lord cardinal."

"But my uncle, Count Armand, is at St. Germain, as sure all Paris knows," Olympia replied, indignantly.

"Ay, 't is so, *ma belle*," young Armand replied, "but they say that the queen will steal away to St. Germain with his little Majesty, and so here come the people in fury to stay her purpose. Hark! there they go again!" and as, before the gates, rose the angry shouts, "The King! the King! Down with Mazarin!" these sprightly young people drew hastily back into the security of their own apartments.

"*Down with Mazarin!*" It was the rallying cry that stirred the excitable people of Paris to riot and violence in those old days of strife and civil war, over two hundred years ago, — the troublesome time of the Fronde. The court of the Queen Regent Anne, the Parliament of Paris, and the great princes of France were struggling for the mastery, in a quarrel so foolish and unnecessary that history has called it "the war of the children," and its very nickname, "the Fronde," was taken from the *fronde*, or sling, which the mischievous boys of Paris used in their heedless street fights. Probably not one half of those who shouted so loudly "Down with Mazarin!" understood what the quarrel was about, nor just why they should rage so violently against the unpopular prime-minister of the queen regent, the Italian Cardinal Mazarin. But they had grown to believe that the scarcity of bread, the pinching pains of hunger, the poverty, and wretchedness which they all *did* understand were due, somehow, to this hated Mazarin, and they were therefore ready to flame up in an instant and to shout "Down with Mazarin!" until they were hoarse.

And now in the great palace all was confusion. Lights flashed from turret to guard-room, casting flickering shadows in the long passages, and gleaming on the gay liveries of the guard as it stood to arms in the gallery where Olympia and Armand had held hurried conversation. Below, the narrow postern opened hastily, and through the swaying and excited crowd pressed the Captain Destouches and his escort of Swiss guards, hurrying with his report to his master, the timorous Duke of Orleans, uncle of the king, and bitter enemy of Mazarin and the regent.

"The King! the King!" rose the people's cry, as they crowded Destouches' little band.

"He is in there," said the guardsman, pointing to the palace.

"Can one see him?" demanded a rough fellow, dashing a flambeau close to the guardsman's face.

Destouches shrugged his shoulders meaningly. "Friend," he said, "I have just seen his little Majesty asleep. Why should not you?"

"The King! the King! We must see the King!" shout the swaying crowd. There is a dash against the trellised gates of the palace, a dash and then a mighty crash, and, as the outer gate falls before the people's assault, the great alarm bell of the palace booms out its note of danger. Then guards and gentlemen press hastily toward the royal apartments in defence of the queen and her sons, while ladies, and pages, and servants scatter and hide in terror.

But Anne, Queen Regent of France, was as brave as she was shrewd.

"What is the people's wish?" she demanded, as the Duc de

Beaufort entered her apartment.

"To see his Majesty with their own eyes, they say," was the reply.

"But can they not trust their queen, my lord?" she asked.

"Their queen, your Highness? Yes. But not Mazarin," said the blunt duke.

"Ho, there, d'Aumont," said the queen to the captain of the palace guard, "bid that the portals be opened at once! Draw off your guard. And you, my lords, stand aside; we will show the king to our good people of Paris and defeat the plots of our enemies. Bid the people enter."

"But — — " said d'Aumont, hesitatingly, fearful as to the result of this concession to the mob.

"Give me no buts!" said Anne, imperiously. "Bid the people enter," and, unattended save by M. de Villeroi, the king's governor, and two of her ladies-in-waiting, she passed quickly through the gallery that led to the magnificent bedchamber of the little King Louis.

"What now, madame?" was the greeting she received from a handsome, auburn-haired boy of twelve, who, as she entered the apartment, was sitting upright in his bed. "Laporte tells me that the rabble are in the palace."

"Lie down, my son," said the queen, "and if ever you seemed to sleep, seem to do so now. Your safety, your crown, perhaps your life, depend upon this masking. The people are crowding the palace, demanding to see with their own eyes that I have not taken you away to St. Germain."

Young Louis of Bourbon flushed angrily. "The people!" he exclaimed. "How dare they? Why does not Villeroi order the Swiss guard to drive the ruffians out?"

"Hush, my Louis," his mother said. "You have other enemies than these barbarians of Paris. Your time has not yet come. Help me play my part and these *frondeurs* may yet feel the force of your sling. Hark, they are here!"

The angry boy dropped upon his pillow and closed his eyes in pretended sleep, while his mother softly opened the door of the apartment, and faced the mob alone. For, obedient to her order, the great portals of the palace had been opened, and up the broad staircase now pushed and scrambled the successful mob. The people were in the palace of the king.

"Enter, my friends," said the intrepid queen, as rough, disordered, and flushed with the novelty of success, the eager crowd halted in presence of royalty. "Enter, my friends; but — softly. The king sleeps. They said falsely who declared that I sought to steal the king from his faithful people of Paris. See for yourselves!" and she swung open the door of the chamber; "here lies your king!" With ready hand she parted the heavy curtains of the splendid bed, and, with finger on lip as if in caution, she beckoned the people to approach the bedside of their boy king.

And then came a singular change. For, as they looked upon the flushed face and the long, disordered hair of that beautiful boy, whose regular breathing seemed to indicate the healthy sleep of childhood, the howling, rebellious rabble of the outer gates became a reverent and loyal throng, which quietly and almost noiselessly filed past the royal bed upon which that strong-willed boy of twelve lay in a "make-believe" sleep.

For two long midnight hours on that memorable tenth of February, 1651, did mother and son endure this trying ordeal. At length it was over. The last burgher had departed, the great gates were closed, the guards were replaced, and, as shouts of "*Vive le roi*" came from the jubilant crowd without, the boy king sprang from his splendid bed and, quivering with shame and rage, shook his little fist toward the cheering people. For, from boyhood, young Louis of Bourbon had been taught to regard himself as the most important lad in all the world. Think, then, what a terrible shock to his pride must have been this invasion of his palace by the people, whom he had been taught to despise.

The angry quarrel of the Fronde raged high for full five months after this midnight reception in the king's bedchamber, but at last came the eventful day which was to fulfil the boy's oft-repeated wish — the day of his majority. For, according to a law of the realm, a king of France could be declared of age at thirteen; and young Louis of Bourbon, naturally a high-spirited lad, had been made even more proud and imperious by his surroundings and education. He chafed under the restraints of the regency, and hailed with delight the day that should set him free.

It was the seventh of August, 1651. Through the echoing streets of Paris wound a glittering cavalcade, gay with streaming banners and a wealth of gorgeous color. With trumpeters in blue velvet and heralds in complete armor, with princes and nobles and high officials mounted on horses gleaming in housings of silver and gold, with horse-guards and foot-guards, pages and attendants, in brilliant uniforms and liveries, rode young King Louis, "Louis the God-given," as his subjects called him, to hold his "Bed of Justice," and proclaim himself absolute king of France. He was a noble-looking young fellow, and he rode his splendid Barbary horse dressed so magnificently that he looked almost "like a golden statue." What wonder that the enthusiastic and loyal Aubery is carried away by his admiration of this kingly boy. "Handsome as Adonis," writes the chronicler. "August in majesty, the pride and joy of humanity, the king looked so tall and majestic that his age would have been thought to be eighteen."

And so through the same mob that five months before had howled around the palace of the imprisoned king, young Louis of Bourbon, rode on to the Palace of Justice while the streets echoed to the loyal shouts of "Vive le roi!" The glittering procession swept into the great hall of the palace and gathered around the throne. And a singular throne it was. On a broad dais, topped with a canopy of crimson and gold, five great cushions were arranged. This was the young king's "Bed of Justice," as it was called. Seating himself upon one cushion, "extending his arms and legs upon three others and using the fifth to lean against," this boy of thirteen, with his plumed and jewelled cap on his head, while every one else remained uncovered, said, in a clear and steady voice: "Messieurs: I have summoned my Parliament to inform its members that, in accordance with the laws of my realm, it is my intention henceforth to assume the government of my kingdom." Then princes and lords, from little "Monsieur," the ten-year-old brother of the king, to the gray old Marshals of France, bent the knee in allegiance, and back to the Palais Royal with his glittering procession, and amid the jubilant shouts of the people, rode the boy king of France, Louis of Bourbon, "King Louis Quatorze."

But alas for the ups and downs of life! This long-wished-for day of freedom did not bring to young Louis the absolute obedience he expected. The struggles of the Fronde still continued, and before the spring of the next year this same haughty young monarch who, in that gorgeous August pageant, had glittered like a "golden statue," found himself with his court, fugitives from Paris, and crowded into stuffy little rooms or uncomfortable old castles, fearful of capture, while not far away the cannons of the two great generals, Turenne and Condé thundered at each other across the Loire, in all the fury of civil war. Something of a bully by nature, for all his blood and kingliness, young Louis seems to have taken a special delight, during these months of wandering, in tormenting his equally high-spirited brother, the little "Monsieur"; and there flashes across the years a very "realistic" picture of a narrow room in the old chateau of Corbeil, in which, upon a narrow bed, two angry boys are rolling and pulling and scratching in a bitter "pillow-fight," brought on by some piece of boyish tyranny on the elder brother's part. And these two boys are not the "frondeurs" of the Paris streets, but the highest dignitaries, of France — her king and her royal prince. There is but little difference in the make-up of a boy, you see, whether he be prince or pauper.

But even intrigue and quarrel may wear themselves out. Court and people alike wearied of the foolish and ineffectual strivings of the Fronde, and so it came about that in the fall of 1652, after a year of exile, the gates of Paris opened to the king, while the unpopular Mazarin, so long the object of public hatred, the man who had been exiled and outlawed, hunted and hounded for years, now returned to Paris as the chief adviser of the boy-king, with shouts of welcome filling the streets that for so many years had resounded with the cry of *"Down with Mazarin!"*

And now the gay court of King Louis Fourteenth blazed forth in all the brilliancy of pomp and pleasure. The boy, himself, as courageous in the trenches and on the battle-field as he was royal and imperious in his audience-chamber, became the hero and idol of the people. Life at his court was very joyous and delightful to the crowd of gay, fun-loving, and unthinking young courtiers who thronged around this powerful young king of fifteen; and not the least brilliant and lively in the royal train were Olympia Mancini and the young Count of Guiche, both proud of their prominence as favorites of the king.

One pleasant afternoon in the early autumn of 1653, a glittering company filled the little theatre of the Hotel de Petit Bourbon, near to the Louvre. The curtain parted, and, now soft and sweet, now fast and furious, the music rose and fell, as the company of amateurs — young nobles and demoiselles of the court — danced, declaimed, and sang through all the mirth and action of one of the lively plays of that period written for the king by Monsieur Benserade.

In one of the numbers of the *ballet*, Mars and Venus stood at the wings awaiting their cue and watching the graceful dancing of a nimble dryad who, beset by a cruel satyr, changed speedily into the tuneful Apollo, vanquished the surprised satyr, and then sang to the accompaniment of his own lute the high-sounding praises of the great and glorious "King Louis Quatorze."

And Mars said to Venus: "Our noble brother Immortal sings divinely; does he not, Olympia? — or thinks he does," he added, in a whisper.

"Hush, Count Armand," Venus replied, holding up a warning finger. "Your last words are barely short of treason."

"Is it treason to tell the truth, fair Olympia?" asked the boy courtier. "Sure, you hear little enough of it from royal lips."

Olympia tossed her pretty head disdainfully. "And how can you know, Sir Count, that his Majesty does not mean truthfully all the pretty things he says to me? Ay, sir, and perhaps — — "

"Well! perhaps what, Mam'selle?" Count Armand asked, as the imperious little lady hesitated in her speech.

"Perhaps — well — who knows? Perhaps, some day, Count Armand, you may rue on bended knee the sharp things you are now so fond of saying to me — to me, who may then be — Olympia, Queen of France!"

Armand laughed softly. "Ho, stands my lady there?" he said. "I kiss your Majesty's hand, and sue for pardon," and he bent in mock reverence above the beautiful hand which the young king admired, and the courtiers, therefore, dutifully raved over. "But — — " he added, slowly.

"But what, Count?" Olympia exclaimed, hastily withdrawing her hand.

"Why, his Majesty says just as many and as pretty things, believe me, to all the fair young demoiselles of his court."

"Ay, but he *means* them with me," the girl protested. "Why, Count, who can stand before me in the king's eyes? Can the little square-nozed Montmorency, or the straw-colored Marie de Villeroi? Can — ah, Count, is it, think you, that very proper little girl sitting there so demurely by her mamma in the *fauteuil* yonder — is it she that may be foremost in the king's thoughts?"

"What, the Princess Henrietta of England?" exclaimed the count. "Ah, no, Olympia; trust me, *le Dieu-donné* looks higher than the poverty-stricken daughter of a headless king and a crownless queen. There is nought to fear from her. But, come, there is our cue," and, with a gay song upon their gossipy lips, Mars and Venus danced in upon the stage, while a terrible Fury circled around them in a mad whirl. And amid the applause of the spectators the three bowed low in acknowledgment, but the Fury received by far the largest share of the *bravas* — for you must know that the nimble dryad, the tuneful Apollo, and the madly whirling Fury were alike his gracious Majesty, Louis, King of France, who was passionately fond of amateur theatricals, sometimes appearing in four or five different characters in a single *ballet*.

That very evening the most select of the court circle thronged the spacious apartments of the queen-mother in attendance at the ball given to the widowed queen of England, who, since the execution of her unfortunate husband, Charles the First, had found shelter at the court of her cousin Louis. And with her came her daughter, the little Princess Henrietta, a fair and timid child of eleven.

The violins sounded the call to places in the *bransle*, the favorite dance of the gay court, and Count Armand noted the smile of triumph which Mam'selle Olympia turned toward him, as King Louis solicited her hand for the dance. And yet she paused before accepting this invitation, for she knew that the honor of opening the dance with the king belonged to the little Henrietta, the guest of the evening. She was still halting between desire and decorum, when Anne, the queen-mother, rising in evident surprise at this uncivil action of her son, stepped down from her seat and quietly withdrew the young girl's hand from that of the king.

"My Louis," she said, in a low voice, "this is but scant courtesy to your cousin and guest, the Princess of England."

The boy's face flushed indignantly at this interference with his wishes, and looking towards the timid Henrietta, he said, with singular rudeness: "'T is not my wish, madame, to dance with the Princess. I am not fond of little girls."

His mother looked at him in quick displeasure. And the Queen of England, who had also heard the ungallant reply, keenly felt her position of dependence on so ungracious a relative, as she hastened to say: "Pardon, dear cousin, but do not, I beg, constrain his Majesty to dance contrary to his wishes. The Princess Henrietta's ankle is somewhat sprained and she can dance but ill."

The imperious nature of Anne of Austria yielded neither to the wishes of a sulky boy nor to the plea of a sprained ankle. "Nay, your Majesty," she said, "I pray you let my desire rule. For, by my word, if the fair Princess of England must remain a simple looker-on at this, my ball, to-night, then, too, shall the King of France."

With a face still full of anger Louis turned away, and when the music again played the opening measures, a weeping little princess and a sulky young king danced in the place of honor. For the poor Henrietta had also overheard the rude words of her mighty cousin of France.

As, after the ball, the king and his mother parted for the night, Anne said to her son: "My dear Louis, what evil spirit of discourtesy led you to so ungallant an action towards your guest, this night? Never again, I beg, let me have need openly to correct so grave a fault."

"Madame," said Louis, turning hotly towards his mother, "who is the lord of France — Louis the King or Anne of Austria?"

The queen started in wonder and indignation at this outburst; but the boy's proud spirit was up, and he continued, despite her protests.

"Too long," he said, "have I been guided by your leading-strings. Henceforth I will be my own master, and do not you, madame, trouble yourself to criticise or correct me. I am the king."

And thus the mother who had sacrificed and suffered so much for the son she idolized found herself overruled by the haughty and arrogant nature she had, herself, done so much to foster. For, from that tearful evening of the queen's ball to the day of his death, sixty-one years after, Louis of Bourbon, called the Great, ruled as absolute lord over his kingdom of France, and the boy who could say so defiantly "Henceforth I will be my own master," was fully equal to that other famous declaration of arrogant authority made, years after, in the full tide of his power, "*I am the state!*"

On the afternoon of an April day in the year 1654 a brilliant company gathered within the old chateau of Vincennes for the royal hunt which was to take place on the morrow. In the great hall all was mirth and fun, as around the room raced king and courtiers in a royal game of "clignemusette" — "Hoodman Blind," or "Blindman's Buff," as we now know it. Suddenly the blindfolded king felt his arm seized, and the young Count of Guiche, who had just entered, whispered: "Sire, here is word from Fouquet that the parliament have moved to reconsider the registry of your decree."

The boy king tore the bandage from his eyes. "How dare they," he said; "how dare they question my demands!"

Now it seems that this decree looked to the raising of money for the pleasures of the king by M. Fouquet, the royal Minister of Finance, and so anxious had Louis been to secure it that he had attended the parliament himself to see that his decree received prompt registry. How dared they then think twice as to the king's wishes?

"Ride you to Paris straight, De Guiche," he said, "and, in the king's name, order that parliament reassemble to-morrow. I will attend their session, and then let them reconsider my decree if they dare!"

Olympia Mancini heard the command of the king. "To-morrow? Oh, sire!" she said; "to-morrow is the royal hunt. How can we spare your Majesty? How Can we give up our sport?"

"Have no fear, mam'selle," said the king, "I will meet my parliament to-morrow, but this trivial business shall not mar our royal hunt. Together will we ride down the stag."

At nine o'clock the next morning parliament re-assembled, as ordered by the king, and the representatives of the people were thunderstruck to see the king enter the great hall of the palace in full hunting costume of scarlet coat, high boots, and plumed gray beaver. Behind him came a long train of nobles in hunting suits also. Whip in hand and hat on head, this self-willed boy of sixteen faced his wondering parliament, and said:

"Messieurs: It has been told me that it is the intention of some members of your body to oppose the registration of my edicts as ordered yesterday. Know now that it is my desire and my will that in future all my edicts shall be registered at once and not discussed. Look you to this; for, should you at any time go contrary to my wish, by my faith, I will come here and enforce obedience!"

Before this bold assertion of mastership the great parliament of Paris bent in passive submission. The money was forthcoming, and in less than an hour the boy king and his nobles were galloping back to Vincennes, and the royal hunt soon swept through the royal forest.

Thus, we see, nothing was permitted to stay the tide of pleasure. Even the battle-field and the siege were turned into spectacles, and, by day and night, the gay court rang with mirth and folly.

In the great space between the Louvre and the Tuileries, since known as the Place de Carrousel, the summer sky of 1654 arched over a gorgeous pageant. Lists and galleries in the fashion of the tournaments of old, fluttering streamers, gleaming decorations, and rich hangings framed a picture that seemed to revive the chivalry of by-gone days. Midway down the lists, in the ladies' gallery, a richly-canopied *fauteuil* or arm-chair, draped in crimson and gold, held the "queen of beauty," the fair-faced Olympia Mancini — the imperious young lady "whom the king delighted to honor." The trumpets of the heralds sounded, and into the lists, with pages and attendants, gallant in liveries of every hue, rode the gay young nobles of the court, gleaming in brilliant costume and device, like knights of old, ready to join in the games of the mock tournament. But the centre of every game, the victor in all the feats of skill and strength, was the boy king, Louis of Bourbon, as in a picturesque suit of scarlet and gold he rode his splendid charger like a statue. And as the spectators noted the white and scarlet scarf that fell from the kingly shoulder in a great band, and the scarlet hat with snow-white plume, they saw, by looking at the fair young "queen of beauty," Olympia Mancini, in her drapery of scarlet damask and white, that King Louis wore her colors, and thus announced himself as her champion in the lists.

And Count Armand could see by the look of triumph and satisfaction in Olympia's pretty face, as she ruled queen of the revels, that already she felt herself not far from the pinnacle of her ambition, and saw herself in the now not distant future as Olympia, Queen of France!

But alas for girlish fancies! Louis, the king, was as fickle in his affections as he was unyielding in his mastership.

"Sire," said the Count de Guiche, as the next day a gay throng rode from the mock tournament to another great hunt in the forest of Vincennes, "why does not the fair Olympia ride with the hunt to-day?"

"Ah, the saucy Mazarinette," the king said, surlily, using the popular nickname given to the nieces of his minister, "she played me a pretty trick last night, and I will have none of her, I say"; and then he told the condoling count, who, however, was in the secret, how at the great ball after the tournament, the maiden, whose colors he had worn, had exchanged suits with his brother, the little "Monsieur," and so cleverly was the masquerading done, that he, the great King Louis, was surprised by the laughing Olympia, making sweet speeches to his own brother, thinking that he was talking to the mischievous maiden.

"My faith, sire," said the laughing count, "Monsieur makes a fair dame when he thus masquerades. Did he not well bear off the character of the Mancini?"

"Pah, all too well, the ugly little *garçon*," ruefully replied the king. "But I gave him such a cuff for his game on me as he shall not soon forget. And as for her — — "

"Well," said the young count, "what did you, sire, to the fair Olympia?"

"Fair, say you?" said the king, wrathfully; "she is aught but fair, say I, Armand — a black face and a black soul! What think you? She strutted forth with all the airs of the great Bayard or — of myself, and clapping hand to sword, she rescued Monsieur from my clutch, saying: 'I am a chevalier of France, and brook no ill usage of so fair a dame!'"

This was too much even for the young courtier, and he burst out a-laughing. But the king was sulky. For Louis of Bourbon, like many a less-titled lad, could enjoy any joke save one played upon himself, and the mischievous Olympia lived to regret her joking of a king. Once at odds with her, the king's fancies flew from one fair damsel to another, finally culminating when, in 1660, he married, for state reasons only, in the splendid palace on the Isle of Pheasants, reared specially for the occasion, the young Princess Maria Theresa, Infanta of Spain, and daughter of his uncle, King Philip the Fourth.

From here the boy merges into the man, and we must leave him. Strong of purpose, clear-headed and masterful, Louis the Fourteenth ruled as King of France for seventy-two years — the most powerful monarch in Christendom. Handsome in person, majestic in bearing, dignified, lavish, and proud; ruling France in one of the most splendid periods of its history — a period styled "the Augustan age" of France; flattered, feared, and absolutely obeyed, one would think, boys and girls, that so powerful a monarch must have been a happy man. But he was not. He lived to see children and grandchildren die around him, to see the armies of France, which he had thought invincible, yield again and again to the superior generalship of Marlborough and Prince Eugene, and to regret with deep remorse the follies and extravagance of his early days. "My child," he said, in his last hours, to his great-grandson and heir, the little five-year-old Louis, "you are about to become a great king; do not imitate me either in my taste for building, or in my love of war. Endeavor, on the contrary, to live in peace with the neighboring nations; render to God all that you owe him, and cause his name to be honored by your subjects. Strive to relieve the burdens of your people, as I, alas! have failed to do."

It is for us to remember that kings and conquerors are often unable to achieve the grandest success of life, — the ruling of themselves, — and that flattery and fear are not the true indications of greatness or of glory. No sadder instance of this in all history is to be found than in the life-story of this cold-hearted, successful, loveless, imperious, all-supreme, and yet friendless old man — one of the world's most powerful monarchs, Louis of Bourbon, Louis "the Great," Louis "the God-given," Louis the

Grande Monarque, Louis the worn-out, unloving and unloved old man of magnificent Versailles.

XI. CHARLES OF SWEDEN: THE BOY CONQUEROR.

(Known as King Charles the Twelfth of Sweden.) A.D. 1699.

In an old, old palace on the rocky height of the *Slottsbacke*, or Palace Hill, in the northern quarter of the beautiful city of Stockholm, the capital of Sweden, there lived, just two hundred years ago, a bright young prince. His father was a stern and daring warrior-king — a man who had been a fighter from his earliest boyhood; who at fourteen had been present in four pitched battles with the Danes; and who, while yet scarce twelve years old, had charged the Danish line at the head of his guards and shot down the stout Danish colonel, who could not resist the spry young warrior; his mother was a sweet-faced Danish princess, a loving and gentle lady, who scarce ever heard a kind word from her stern-faced husband, and whose whole life was bound up in her precious little prince.

And this little Carolus, Karl, or Charles, dearly loved his tender mother. From her he learned lessons of truth and nobleness that even through all his stormy and wandering life never forsook him. Often while he had swung gently to and fro in his quaint, carved, and uncomfortable-looking cradle, had she crooned above him the old saga-songs that told of valor and dauntless courage and all the stern virtues that made up the heroes of those same old saga-songs. Many a time she had trotted the little fellow on her knee to the music of the ancient nursery rhyme that has a place in all lands and languages, from the steppes of Siberia to the homes of New York and San Francisco:

"Ride along, ride a cock-horse,
His mane is dapple-gray;
Ride along, ride a cock-horse,

Little boy, ride away.
Where shall the little boy ride to?
To the king's court to woo" — —

and so forth, and so forth, and so forth — in different phrases but with the same idea, as many and many a girl and boy can remember. And she had told him over and over again the saga-stories and fairy tales that every Scandinavian boy and girl, from prince to peasant, knows so well — of Frithiof and Ingeborg, and the good King Rene; and about the Stone Giant and his wife Guru; and how the Bishop's cattle were turned into mice; and about the dwarfs, and trolls, and nixies, and beautiful mermaids and stromkarls. And she told him also many a story of brave and daring deeds, of noble and knightly lives, and how his ancestors, from the great Gustavus, and, before, from the still greater Gustavus Vasa, had been kings of Sweden, and had made the name of that northern land a power in all the courts of Europe.

Little Prince Charles was as brave as he was gentle and jolly, and as hardy as he was brave. At five years old he killed his first fox; at seven he could manage his horse like a young centaur; and at twelve he had his first successful bear hunt. He was as obstinate as he was hardy; he steadily refused to learn Latin or French — the languages of the court — until he heard that the kings of Denmark and Poland understood them, and then he speedily mastered them.

His lady-mother's death, when he was scarce twelve years old, was a great sadness, and nearly caused his own death, but, recovering his health, he accompanied his father on hunting parties and military expeditions, and daily grew stronger and hardier than ever.

In April, 1697, when the Prince was not yet fifteen, King Charles the Eleventh, his stern-faced father, suddenly died, and the boy king succeeded to the throne as absolute lord of "Sweden and Finland, of Livonia, Carelia, Ingria, Wismar, Wibourg, the islands of Rugen and Oesel, of Pomerania, and the duchies of Bremen and Verdun," — one of the finest possessions to which a young king ever succeeded, and representing what is now Sweden, Western Russia, and a large part of Northern Germany.

A certain amount of restraint is best for us all. As the just restraints of the law are best for men and women, so the proper restraints of home are best for boys and girls. A lad from whom all restraining influences are suddenly withdrawn — who can have his own way unmolested, — stands in the greatest danger of wrecking his life. The temptations of power have been the cause of very much of the world's sadness and misery. And this temptation came to this boy king of Sweden, called in his fifteenth year to supreme sway over a large realm of loyal subjects. Freed from the severity of his stern father's discipline, he found himself responsible to no one — absolutely his own master. And he did what too many of us, I fear, would have done, in his position — he determined to have a jolly good time, come what might; and he had it — in his way.

He and his brother-in-law, the wild young Duke of Holstein, turned the town upside down. They snapped cherry pits at the king's gray-bearded councillors, and smashed in the windows of the staid and scandalized burghers of Stockholm. They played ball with the table dishes, and broke all the benches in the palace chapel. They coursed hares through the council-chambers of the Parliament House, and ran furious races until they had ruined several fine horses. They beheaded sheep in the palace till the floors ran with blood, and then pelted the passers-by with sheep's heads. They spent the money in the royal treasury like water, and played so many heedless and ruthless boy-tricks that the period of these months of folly was known, long after, as the "Gottorp Fury," because the harum-scarum young brother-in-law, who was the ringleader in all these scrapes, was Duke of Holstein-Gottorp.

But at last, even the people — serfs of this boy autocrat though they were — began to murmur, and when one Sunday morning three clergymen preached from the text: "Woe to thee, O land, when thy king is a child," the young sovereign remembered the counsels of his good mother and recalled the glories of his ancestors, saw how foolish and dangerous was all this reckless sport, turned over a new leaf, became thoughtful and care-taking, and began his career of conquest with the best victory of all — the conquest of himself!

But though he curbed his tendency to profitless and hurtful "skylarking," he had far too much of the Berserker blood of his ancestors — those rough old vikings who "despised mail and helmet and went into battle unharnessed" — to become altogether gentle in manners or occupation. He hated his fair skin, and sought in every way to tan and roughen it, and to harden himself by exposure and neglect of personal comfort. Many a night was passed by the boy on the bare floor, and for three nights in the cold Swedish December he slept in the hay-loft of the palace stables, without undressing and with but a scanty covering.

So he grew to be a lad of seventeen, sturdy, strong, and hardy, and at the date of our story, in the year 1699, the greater part of his time was given up to military exercises and field sports, with but little attention to debates in council or to the cares of state.

Among his chief enjoyments were the sham fights on land and water. Many a hard-fought battle was waged between the boys and young men who made up his guards and crews, and who would be divided into two or more opposing parties, as the plan of battle required. This was rough and dangerous sport, and was attended often with really serious results. But the participants were stout and sturdy Northern lads, used to hardships and trained to physical endurance. They thought no more of these encounters than do the boys of to-day of the crush of football and the hard hitting of the base-ball field, and blows were given and taken with equal good nature and unconcern.

One raw day in the early fall of 1699, sturdy young Arvid Horn, a stout, blue-eyed Stockholm boy, stripped to the waist, and with a gleam of fun in his eyes, stood upright in his little boat as it bobbed on the crest of the choppy Maelar waves. He hailed the king's yacht.

"Holo; in the boat there! Stand for your lives!" he shouted, and levelled his long squirt-gun full at the helmsman.

Swish! came the well-directed stream of water plump against

the helmsman's face. Again and again it flew, until dripping and sore he dropped the tiller and dashed down the companion-way calling loudly for help.

Help came speedily, and as the crew of the king's yacht manned the rail and levelled at their single assailant the squirt-guns, which were the principal weapons of warfare used in these "make-believe" naval engagements, the fun grew fast and furious; but none had so sure an aim or so strong an arm to send an unerring and staggering stream as young Arvid Horn. One by one he drove them back, while as his boat drifted still nearer the yacht he made ready to spring to the forechains and board his prize. But even before he could steady himself for the jump, another tall and fair-haired Stockholm lad, darting out from the high cabin, rallied the defeated crew and bade them man the pumps at once.

A clumsy-looking fire-engine stood amidship, and the crew leaped to its pumps as directed, while the new-comer, catching up a line of hose, sprang to the rail and sent a powerful stream of water straight against the solitary rover.

"Repel boarders!" he cried, laughingly, and the sudden stream from the fire-engine's nozzle sent young Arvid Horn staggering back into his boat.

But he rallied quickly, and with well-charged squirt-gun attacked the new defender of the yacht. The big nozzle, however, was more than a match for the lesser squirt-gun, and the small boat speedily began to fill under the constant deluge of water from the engine.

"Yield thee, yield thee, Arvid Horn; yield thee to our unconquerable nozzle," came the summons from the yacht; "yield thee, or I will drown you out like a rat in a cheese-press!"

"Arvid Horn yields to no one," the plucky boy in the boat made answer, and with a parting shot and a laughing "*Farväl*" he leaped from the sinking boat into the dancing Maelar water. Striking boldly out he swam twice round the boat in sheer bravado, defying the enemy; now ducking to escape the pursuing stream, or now, while floating on his back, sending a return shot with telling force against the men at the pump — for he still clung to his trusty squirt-gun.

The fair-faced lad in the yacht looked at the swimmer in evident admiration.

"Is it, then, hard to swim, Arvid Horn?" he inquired.

"Not if one is fearless," called back the floating boy.

"How; fearless?" exclaimed the lad on the yacht, hastily. "Do you perhaps think that I am afraid?"

"I said not so," replied young Arvid, coolly sending a full charge from his squirt-gun straight up in air.

"No; but you mean it — good faith, you mean it then," said the lad, and flinging off wig, cocked hat, and long coat only, without an instant's hesitation, he, too, leaped into the Maelar lake.

There is nothing so cooling to courage or reckless enthusiasm as cold water — if one cannot swim. The boy plunged and floundered, and, weighty with his boots and his clothing, soon sank from sight. As he came spluttering to the surface again, "Help, help, Arvid," he called despairingly; "I am drowning!"

Arvid, who had swum away from his friend, thinking that he would follow after, heard the cry and caught a still louder one from the yacht: "The king, the king is sinking!"

A few strokes brought him near to the over-confident diver, and clutching him by his shirt collar, he kept the lad's head above water until, after a long and laborious swim, he brought his kingly burden safe to land — for the fair-haired and reckless young knight of the nozzle was none other than His Gracious Majesty, Charles the Twelfth of Sweden.

"Truly it is one thing to be brave and another to be skilful," said the king, as he stood soaked and dripping on the shore. "But for you, friend Arvid, I had almost gone."

"You are very wet, sire, and may take cold," said Arvid, "let us hasten at once to yonder house for warmth and dry clothes."

"Not so, Arvid; I do not fear the water — on land," said the king. "I am no such milksop as to need to dry off before a kitchen fire. See, this is the better way;" and catching up a stout hazel-stick, he bade Arvid stand on his guard. Nothing loth, Arvid Horn accepted the kingly challenge, and picking up a similar hazel-stick, he rapped King Charles' weapon smartly, and the two boys went at each other "hammer and tongs" in a lively bout at "single-stick."

They were soon thoroughly warmed up by this vigorous exercise, and forgot their recent bath and the king's danger. It was a drawn battle, however, and, as they paused for breath, King Charles said: "Trust that to drive away cold and ague, Arvid. Faith, 't is a rare good sport."

"Could it be done on horseback, think you?" queried Arvid, always on the look-out for sensation.

"And why not? 'T is well thought," said the king. "Let us straight to the palace yard and try it for ourselves."

But ere they reached the palace the idea had developed into still greater proportions.

The king's guards were summoned, and divided into two parties. Their horses were unsaddled, and, riding "bareback" and armed with nothing but hazel-sticks, the two forces were pitted against each other in a great cavalry duel of "single-stick."

King Charles commanded one side, and young Arvid Horn the other. At it they went, now one side and now the other having the advantage, the two leaders fighting with especial vigor.

Arvid pressed the king closely, and both lads were full of the excitement of the fray when Charles, careless of his aim and with his customary recklessness, brought his hazel-stick with a terrible thwack upon poor Arvid's face. Now, Arvid Horn had a boil on his cheek, and if any of my boy readers know what a tender piece of property a boil is, they will know that King Charles' hazel-stick was not a welcome poultice.

With a cry of pain Arvid fell fainting from his horse, and the cavalry battle at "single-stick" came to a sudden stop. But the heat and the pain brought on so fierce a fever that the lad was soon as near to death's door as his friend King Charles had been in the sea fight of the squirt-guns.

The king was deeply concerned during young Arvid's illness, and when the lad at last recovered, he made him a present of two thousand thalers, laughingly promising to repeat the prescription whenever Arvid was again wounded at "single-stick." He was greatly pleased to have his friend with him once more, and, when Arvid was strong enough to join in his vigorous sports again, one of the first things he proposed was a great bear-hunt up among the snow-filled forests that skirted the Maelar Lake.

A day's ride from Stockholm, the hunting-lodge of the kings of Sweden lay upon the heavily drifted hill-slopes just beyond the lake shore, and through the forests and marshes two hundred years ago the big brown bear of Northern Europe, the noble elk, the now almost extinct aurochs, or bison, and the great gray wolf roamed in fierce and savage strength, affording exciting and dangerous sport for daring hunters.

And among these hunters none excelled young Charles of Sweden. Reckless in the face of danger, and brave as he was reckless, he was ever on the alert for any novelty in the manner of hunting that should make the sport even more dangerous and exciting. So young Arvid Horn was not surprised when the king said to him:

"I have a new way for hunting the bear, Arvid, and a rarely good one too."

"Of that I'll be bound, sire," young Arvid responded; "but — how may it be?"

"You shall know anon," King Charles replied; "but this much will I say: I do hold it but a coward's part to fight the poor brute with fire-arms. Give the fellow a chance for his life, say I, and a fair fight in open field — and then let the best man win."

Here was a new idea. Not hunt the bear with musket, carbine, or wheel-lock? What then — did King Charles reckon to have a wrestling bout or a turn at "single-stick" with the *Jarl* Bruin? So wondered Arvid Horn, but he said nothing, waiting the king's own pleasure, as became a shrewd young courtier.

And soon enough he learned the boy-hunter's new manner of bear-hunting, when, on the very day of their arrival at the Maelar lodge, they tracked a big brown bear beneath the great pines and spruces of the almost boundless forest, armed only with strong wooden pitchforks. Arvid was not at all anxious for this fighting at close quarters, but when he saw King Charles boldly advance upon the growling bear, when he saw the great brute rise on his hind legs and threaten to hug Sweden's monarch to death, he would have sprung forward to aid his king. But a huntsman near at hand held him back.

"Wait," said the man; "let the 'little father' play his part."

And even as he spoke Arvid saw the king walk deliberately up to the towering bear, and, with a quick thrust of his long-handled fork, catch the brute's neck between the pointed wooden prongs, and with a mighty shove, force the bear backward in the snow.

Then, answering his cry of "Holo, all!" the huntsmen sprang to his side, flung a stout net over the struggling bear, and held it thus, a floundering prisoner, while the intrepid king coolly cut its throat with his sharp hunting-knife.

Arvid learned to do this too in time, but it required some extra courage even for his steady young head and hand.

One day when each of the lads had thus transfixed and killed his bear, and as, in high spirits, they were returning to the hunting-lodge, a courserman dashed hurriedly across their path, recognized the king, and reining in his horse, dismounted hastily, saluted, and handed the king a packet.

"From the council, sire," he said.

Up to this day the young king had taken but little interest in the affairs of state, save as he directed the review or drill, leaving the matters of treaty and of state policy to his trusted councillors.

He received the courserman's despatch with evident unconcern, and read it carelessly. But his face changed as he read it a second time; first clouding darkly, and then lighting up with the gleam of a new determination and purpose.

"What says Count Piper?" he exclaimed half aloud; "Holstein laid waste by Denmark, Gottorp Castle taken, and the Duke a fugitive? And my council dares to temper and negotiate? *Ack; so!* Arvid Horn, we must be in Stockholm ere nightfall."

"But, sire, how can you?" exclaimed Arvid. "The roads are heavy with snow, and no horse could stand the strain or hope to make the city ere morning."

"No horse!" cried King Charles; "then three shall do it. Hasten; bid Hord the equerry harness the triple team to the strongest sledge, and be you ready to ride with me in a half hour's time. For we shall be in Stockholm by nightfall."

And ere the half hour was up they were off. Careless of roadway, straight for Stockholm they headed, the triple team of plunging Ukraine horses, driven abreast by the old equerry Hord, dashing down the slopes and across the Maelar ice, narrowly escaping collision, overturn, and death. With many a plunge and many a ducking, straight on they rode, and ere the Stockholm clocks had struck the hour of six, the city gates were passed, and the spent and foaming steeds dashed panting into the great yard of the Parliament House.

The council was still in session, and the grave old councillors started to their feet in amazement at this sudden apparition of the boy king, soiled and bespattered from head to foot, standing there in their midst.

"Gentlemen," he said, with earnestness and determination in his voice, "your despatch tells me of unfriendly acts on the part of the king of Denmark against our brother and ally of Holstein-Gottorp. I am resolved never to begin an unjust war, but never to finish an unjust one save with the destruction of mine enemies. My resolution is fixed. I will march and attack the first one who shall declare war; and when I shall have conquered him, I hope to strike terror into the rest."

These were ringing and, seemingly, reckless words for a boy of seventeen, and we do not wonder that, as the record states, "the old councillors, astonished at this declaration, looked at each other without daring to answer." The speech seemed all the more reckless when they considered, as we may here, the coalition against which the boy king spoke so confidently.

At that time — in the year 1699 — the three neighbors of this young Swedish monarch were three kings of powerful northern nations — Frederick the Fourth, King of Denmark, Augustus, called the Strong, King of Poland and Elector of Saxony, and Peter, afterward known as the Great, Czar of Russia. Tempted by the large possessions of young King Charles, and thinking to take advantage of his youth, his inexperience, and his presumed indifference, these three monarchs concocted a fine scheme by which Sweden was to be overrun, conquered, and divided among the three members of this new copartnership of kings — from each of whom, or from their predecessors, this boy king's ancestors had wrested many a fair domain and wealthy city.

But these three kings — as has many and many another plotter in history before and since — reckoned without their host. They did not know the mettle that was in this grandnephew of the great Gustavus.

Once aroused to action, he was ready to move before even his would-be conquerors, in those slow-going days, imagined he had thought of resistance. Money and men were raised, the alliance of England and Holland were secretly obtained, a council of defence was appointed to govern Sweden during the absence of the king, and on the twenty-third of April, 1700, two months before his eighteenth birthday, King Charles bade his grandmother and his sisters good-bye and left Stockholm for ever.

Even as he left the news came that another member in this firm of hostile kings, Augustus of Saxony and Poland, had invaded Sweden's tributary province of Livonia on the Gulf of Finland. Not to be drawn aside from his first object — the punishment of Denmark — Charles simply said: "We will make King

Augustus go back the way he came," and hurried on to join his army in Southern Sweden.

By the third of August, 1700, King Charles had grown tired of waiting for his reserves and new recruits, and so, with scarce six thousand men, he sailed away from Malmo — clear down at the most southerly point of Sweden — across the Sound, and steered for the Danish coast not twenty-five miles away.

Young Arvid Horn, still the king's fast friend, and now one of his aids, following his leader, leaped into the first of the small barges or row-boats that were to take the troops from the frigates to the Danish shore. His young general and king, impatient at the slowness of the clumsy barges, while yet three hundred yards from shore, stood upright in the stern, drew his sword, and exclaimed: "I am wearied with this pace. All you who are for Denmark follow me!" And then, sword in hand, he sprang over into the sea.

Arvid Horn quickly followed his royal friend. The next moment generals and ministers, ambassadors and belaced officials, with the troops that filled the boats, were wading waist-deep through the shallow water of the Sound, struggling toward the Danish shore, and fully as enthusiastic as their hasty young leader and king.

The Danish musket-balls fell thick around them as the Danish troops sought from their trenches to repel the invaders.

"What strange whizzing noise is this in the air?" asked the young king, now for the first time in action.

"'T is the noise of the musket-balls they fire upon you," was the reply.

"*Ack*, say you so," said Charles; "good, good; from this time forward that shall be my music."

In the face of this "music" the shore was gained, the trenches were carried by fierce assault, and King Charles' first battle was won. Two days later, Copenhagen submitted to its young conqueror, and King Frederick, of Denmark, hastened to the defence of his capital, only to find it in the possession of the enemy, and to sign a humiliating treaty of peace.

The boy conqueror's first campaign was over, and, as his biographer says, he had "at the age of eighteen begun and finished a war in less than six weeks." Accepting nothing for himself from this conquest, he spared the land from which his dearly-remembered mother had come, from the horrors of war and pillage which, in those days, were not only allowable but expected.

King Augustus, of Poland, seeing the short work made of his ally, the king of Denmark, by this boy king, whom they had all regarded with so much contempt, deemed discretion to be the better part of valor and, as the lad had prophesied, withdrew from Livonia, "going back by the way he came." Then the young conqueror, flushed with his successes, turned his army against his third and greatest enemy, Czar Peter, of Russia, who, with over eighty thousand men, was beseiging the Swedish town of Narva.

A quaint old German-looking town, situated a few miles from the shores of the Gulf of Finland, in what is now the Baltic provinces of Russia, and near to the site of the Czar's later capital of St. Petersburg, the stout-walled town of Narva was the chief defence of Sweden on its eastern borders, and a stronghold which the Russian monarch especially coveted for his own. Young Arvid Horn's uncle, the Count Horn, was in command of the Swedish forces in the town, which, with a thousand men, he held for the young king, his master, against all the host of the Czar Peter.

Eagle-Flag Of Sweden.

The boy who had conquered Denmark in less than six weeks, and forced a humiliating peace from Poland, was not the lad to consider for a moment the question of risk or of outnumbering forces. In the middle of November, when all that cold Northern land is locked in ice and snow, he flung out the eagle-flag of Sweden to the Baltic blasts, and crossed to the instant relief of Narva, with an army of barely twenty thousand men. Landing at Pernau with but a portion of his troops, he pushed straight on, and with scarce eight thousand men, hurried forward to meet the enemy. With a courage as daring as his valor was headlong he surprised and routed first one and then another advance detachment of the Russian force, and soon twenty-five thousand demoralized and defeated men were retreating before him, into the Russian camp. In less than two days all the Russian outposts were carried, and on the noon of the 30th of November, 1700, the boy from Sweden appeared with his eight thousand victory-flushed though wearied troops before the fortified camp of his enemy, and, without a moment's hesitation, ordered instant battle.

"Sire," said one of his chief officers, the General Stenbock, "do you comprehend the greatness of our danger? The Muscovites outnumber us ten to one."

"What! then," said the intrepid young king, "do you imagine that with my eight thousand brave Swedes I shall not be able to march over the bodies of eighty thousand Muscovites?" and then at the signal of two fusees and the watchword, "With the help of God," he ordered his cannon to open on the Russian trenches, and through a furious snow-storm charged straight upon the enemy.

Again valor and enthusiasm triumphed. The Russian line broke before the impetuosity of the Swedes, and, as one chronicler says, "ran about like a herd of cattle"; the bridge across the river broke under the weight of fugitives, panic followed, and when night fell the great Russian army of eighty thousand men surrendered as prisoners of war to a boy of eighteen with but eight thousand tired soldiers at his back.

So the boy conqueror entered upon his career of victory. Space does not permit to detail his battles and his conquests. How he placed a new king on the throne of Poland, kept Denmark in submission, held the hosts of Russia at bay, humbled Austria, and made his name, ere yet he was twenty, at once a wonder and a terror in all the courts of Europe. How, at last, his ambition getting the better of his discretion, he thought to be a modern Alexander, to make Europe Protestant, subdue Rome, and carry his conquering eagles into Egypt and Turkey and Persia. How, by unwise measures and fool-hardy endeavors, he lost all the fruits of his hundred victories and his nine years of conquest in the terrible defeat by the Russians at Pultowa, which sent him an exile into Turkey, kept him there a prisoner of state for over five years; and how, finally, when once again at the head of Swedish troops, instead of defending his own home-land of Sweden, he invaded Norway in the depth of winter, and was killed, when but thirty-six, by a cannon shot from the enemy's batteries at Frederickshall on the 11th of December, 1718.

Charles the Twelfth of Sweden was one of the most remarkable of the world's Historic Boys. Elevated to a throne founded on despotic power and victorious memories, at an age when most lads regard themselves as the especial salt of the earth, he found himself launched at once into a war with three powerful nations, only to become in turn the conqueror of each. A singularly good boy, so far as the customary temptations of power and high station are concerned — temperate, simple, and virtuous in tastes, dress, and habits, — he was, as one of his biographers has remarked, "the only one among kings who had lived without a single frailty."

But this valorous boy, who had first bridled his own spirit, and then conquered the Northern world, "reared," as has been said, "under a father cold and stern, defectively educated, taught from childhood to value nothing but military glory," could not withstand the temptation of success. An ambition to be somebody and to do something is always a laudable one in boy or girl, until it supplants and overgrows the sweet, true, and manly boy and girl nature, and makes us regardless of the comfort or the welfare of others. A desire to excel the great conquerors of old, joined to an obstinacy as strong as his courage, caused young Charles of Sweden to miss the golden opportunity, and instead of seeking to rule his own country wisely, sent him abroad a homeless wanderer on a career of conquest, as romantic as it was, first, glorious, and at the last disastrous.

In the northern quarter of the beautiful city of Stockholm, surrounded by palaces and gardens, theatres, statues, and fountains, stands Molin's striking statue of the boy conqueror, Charles the Twelfth of Sweden. Guarded at the base by captured mortars, the outstretched hand and unsheathed sword seem to tell of conquests to be won and victories to be achieved. But to the boy and girl of this age of peace and good fellowship, when wars are averted rather than sought, and wise statesmanship looks rather to the healing than to the opening of the world's wounds, one cannot but feel how much grander, nobler, and more helpful would have been the life of this young "Lion of the North," as his Turkish captors called him, had it been devoted to deeds of gentleness and charity rather than of blood and sorrow, and how much more enduring might have been his fame and his memory if he had been the lover and helper of his uncultivated and civilization-needing people, rather than the valorous, ambitious, headstrong, and obstinate Boy Conqueror of two centuries ago.

XII. Van Rensselaer Of Rensselaerswyck: The Boy Patroon.

(Afterward Major-General, and Lieutenant-Governor of the State of New York.) A.D. 1777.

I question whether any of my young readers, however well up in history they may be, can place the great River of Prince Maurice (*De Riviere Van den Voorst Mauritius*), which, two hundred years ago, flowed through the broad domain of the lord patroons of Rensselaerswyck. And yet it is the same wide river upon whose crowded shore now stands the great city of New York; the same fair river above whose banks now towers the noble front of the massive State Capitol at Albany. And that lofty edifice stands not far from the very spot where, beneath the pyramidal belfry of the old Dutch church, the boy patroon sat nodding through Dominie Westerlo's sermon, one drowsy July Sunday in the summer of 1777.

The good dominie's "seventhly" came to a sudden stop as the tinkle of the deacon's collection-bell fell upon the ears of the slumbering congregation. In the big Van Rensselaer pew it roused Stephanus, the boy patroon, from a delightful dream of a ten-pound *twaalf*, or striped bass, which he thought he had just hooked at the mouth of Bloemert's Kill; and, rather guiltily, as one who has been "caught napping," he dropped his two "half-joes" into the deacon's "fish-net" — for so the boys irreverently called the knitted bag which, stuck on one end of a long pole, was always passed around for contributions right in the middle of the sermon. Then the good dominie went back to his "seventhly," and the congregation to their slumbers, while the restless young Stephanus traced with his finger-nail upon the cover of his psalm-book the profile of his highly respected guardian, General Ten Broek, nodding solemnly in the magistrate's pew. At last, the sands in the hour-glass, that stood on the queer, one-legged, eight-sided pulpit, stopped running, and so did the dominie's "noble Dutch"; the congregation filed out of church, and the Sunday service was over. And so, too, was the Sunday quiet. For scarcely had the people passed the porch, when, down from the city barrier at the Colonie Gate, clattered a hurrying horseman.

"From General Schuyler, sir," he said, as he reined up before General Ten Broek, and handed him an order to muster the militia at once and repair to the camp at Fort Edward. St. Clair, so said the despatch, had been defeated, Ticonderoga was captured, Burgoyne was marching to the Hudson, the Indians were on the war-path, and help was needed at once if they would check Burgoyne and save Albany from pillage.

The news fell with a sudden shock upon the little city of the Dutchmen. Ticonderoga fallen, and the Indians on the war-path! Even the most stolid of the Albany burghers felt his heart beating faster, while many a mother looked anxiously at her little ones and called to mind the terrible tales of Indian cruelty and pillage.

But the young Van Rensselaer, pressing close to the side of fair Mistress Margarita Schuyler, said soberly: "These be sad tidings, Margery; would it not be wiser for you all to come up to the manor-house for safety?"

"For safety?" echoed high-spirited Mistress Margery. "Why, what need, Stephanus? Is not my father in command at Fort Edward? and not for Burgoyne and all his Indians need we fear while he is there! So, many thanks, my lord patroon," she continued, with a mock courtesy; "but I'm just as safe under the Schuyler gables as I could be in the Van Rensselaer manor-house, even with the brave young patroon himself as my defender."

The lad looked a little crestfallen; for he regarded himself as the natural protector of this brave little lady, whose father was facing the British invaders on the shores of the Northern lakes. Had it not been one, almost, of the unwritten laws of the *colonie*, since the day of the first patroon, that a Van Rensselaer should wed a Schuyler? Who, then, should care for a daughter of the house of Schuyler in times of trouble but a son of the house of Rensselaer?

"Well, at any rate, I shall look out for you if danger does come," he said, as he turned toward the manor-house. "You'll surely not object to that, will you, Margery?"

"Why, how can I?" laughed the girl. "I certainly may not prevent a gallant youth from keeping his eyes in my direction. So, thanks for your promise, my lord patroon, and when you see the flash of the tomahawk, summon your vassals like a noble knight and charge through the Colonie Gate to the rescue of the beleaguered maiden of the Fuyck. [38] Why, it will be as good as one of Dominie Westerlo's Northland saga-tales, won't it, Stephanus?" And, with a stately good-by to the little lord of seven hundred thousand acres, the girl hastened homeward to the Schuyler mansion, while the boy rode in the opposite direction to the great brick manor-house by the creek.

Twenty-four miles east and west, by forty-eight miles north and south, covering forest and river, valley and hill, stretched the broad *colonie* of the patroons of Rensselaerswyck, embracing the present counties of Albany, Rensselaer, and Columbia, in the State of New York; and over all this domain, since the days of the Heer Killian Van Rensselaer, first of the lord patroons, father and son, in direct descent, had held sway after the manner of the old feudal barons of Europe. They alone owned the land, and their hundreds of tenants held their farms on rentals or leases, subject to the will of the "patroons," as they were called, — a Dutch adaptation of the old Roman *patronus*, meaning patrician or patron.

Only the town-lands of Beverwyck, or Albany, were free from this feudal right — a territory stretching thirteen miles north-west, by one mile wide along the river front, and forced from an earlier boy patroon by the doughty Peter Stuyvesant, and secured by later English governors; and at the time of our story, though the old feudal laws were no longer in force, and the rentals were less exacting than in the earlier days, the tenantry of Rensselaerswyck respected the authority and manorial rights of Stephen Van Rensselaer, their boy patroon, who, with his widowed mother and his brothers and sisters, lived in the big brick manor-house near the swift mill creek and the tumbling falls in the green vale of Tivoli, a mile north of the city gate.

And now had come the Revolution. Thanks to the teaching of his tender mother, of his gallant guardian, and of the good Dominie Westerlo, young Stephen knew what the great struggle meant — a protest against tyranny, a blow for human rights, a defence of the grand doctrine of the immortal Declaration that "All men are created free and equal." And he had been told, too, that the success of the Republic would be the death-blow to all the feudal rights to which he, the last of the patroons, had succeeded.

"Uncle," he said to his guardian, that stern patriot and whig, General Abram Ten Broek, "you are my representative and must act for me till I grow to be a man. Do what is best, sir, and don't let the Britishers beat!"

"But, remember, lad," said his uncle, "the Revolution, if it succeeds, must strip you of all the powers and rights that have come to you as patroon. You will be an owner of acres, nothing more; no longer baron, patroon, nor lord of the manor; of no higher dignity and condition than little Jan Van Woort, the cowboy of old Luykas Oothout on your cattle farm in the Helderbergs."

"But I'll be a citizen of a free republic, won't I, Uncle?" said the boy; "as free of the king and his court across the sea as Jan Van Woort will be of me and the court-leet of Rensselaerswyck. So we'll all start fair and even. I'm not old enough to fight and talk yet, Uncle; but do you fight and talk for me, and I know it will come out all right."

And so, through the battle-summer of 1777, the work went on. Men and supplies were hurried northward to help the patriot army, and soon General Ten Broek's three thousand militia-men were ready and anxious for action. The air was full of stirring news. Brandt and his Indians, Sir John Johnson and his greencoated Tories, swarmed into the Mohawk Valley; poor Jane McCrea fell a victim to Indian treachery, and the whole northern country shuddered at the rumor that twenty dollars had been offered for every rebel scalp. And fast upon these came still other tidings. The noble General Schuyler, fair Mistress Margery's father, had, through the management of his enemies in the Congress and in the camp, been superseded by General Gates; but, like a true patriot, he worked just as hard for victory nevertheless. Herkimer had fallen in the savage and uncertain fight at Oriskany; in Bennington, stout old Stark had dealt the British a rousing blow; and Burgoyne's boast that with ten thousand men he could "promenade through America" ended dismally enough for him in the smoke of Bemis Heights and the surrender at Saratoga.

But, before that glorious ending, many were the dark and doubtful days that came to Albany and to Rensselaerswyck. Rumors of defeat and disaster, of plot and pillage, filled the little city. Spies and Tories sought to work it harm. The flash of the tomahawk, of which Mistress Margery had so lightly jested, was really seen in the Schuyler mansion. And the brave girl, by her pluck and self-possession, had saved her father and his household from the chance of Tory pillage and Indian murder. Good Dominie Westerlo kept open church and constant prayer for the success of the patriot arms through one whole anxious week, and on a bright September afternoon, General Ten Broek, with a slender escort, came dashing up to the "stoop" of the Van Rensselaer manor-house.

"What now, Uncle?" asked young Stephen, as he met the General in the broad hall.

"More supplies — we must have more supplies, lad," replied his uncle. "Our troops need provisions, and I am here to forage among both friends and foes."

"Beginning with us, I suppose," said the young patroon. "Oh, Uncle, cannot I, too, do something to show my love for the cause?"

"Something, Stephen? You can do much," his uncle replied. "Time was, lad, when your ancestors, the lord patroons of Rensselaerswyck, were makers and masters of the law in this their *colonie*. From their own forts floated their own flag and frowned their own cannon. Their word was law and from Beeren's Island to Pafraet's Dael the Heer Van Rensselaer's orders were obeyed without question. Forts and flags and cannon are no longer yours, Stephen, and we would not have it otherwise; but your word still holds as good with your tenantry as did that of the first boy patroon, Johannes the son of Killian, when, backed by his *gecommitteerden* and his *schepens*, [39] he bearded the Heer General Stuyvesant and claimed all Rensselaerswyck as his 'by right of arms.' Try your word with them, lad. Let me be your *gecommitteerden* and, in the name of the patroon, demand from your tenantry of Rensselaerswyck provisions and forage for our gallant troops."

"Oh, try it, Uncle, try it — do," young Stephen cried, full of interest; "but will they give so much heed, think you, to my word?"

"Ay, trust them for that," replied the general. "So strong is their attachment to their young patroon that they will, I know, do more on your simple word than on all the orders and levies of the king's Parliament or the Continental Congress."

So, out into the farm-lands that checkered the valley and

climbed the green slopes of the Helderbergs, went the orders of the boy patroon, summoning all "our loyal and loving tenantry" to take of their stock and provender all that they could spare, save the slight amount needed for actual home use, and to deliver the same to the commissaries of the army of the Congress at Saratoga. And the "loyal and loving tenantry" gave good heed to their patroon's orders. Granaries and cellars, stables and pigsties, pork-barrels and poultry-sheds, were emptied of their contents. The army of the Congress was amply provisioned, and thus, indeed, did the boy patroon contribute his share toward the great victory at Saratoga — a victory of which one historian remarks that "no martial event, from the battle of Marathon to that of Waterloo — two thousand years, — exerted a greater influence upon human affairs."

The field of Saratoga is won. Six thousand British troops have laid down their arms, and the fears of Northern invasion are ended. In the Schuyler mansion at Albany, fair Mistress Margery is helping her mother fitly entertain General Burgoyne and the paroled British officers, thus returning good for evil to the man who, but a few weeks before, had burned to the ground her father's beautiful country-house at Saratoga. Along the fair river, from the Colonie Gate to the peaks of the Katzbergs, the early autumn frosts are painting the forest leaves with gorgeous tints, and to-day, the first of November, 1777, the children are joyously celebrating the thirteenth birthday of the boy patroon in the big manor-house by the creek. For, in Albany, a hundred years ago, a children's birthday party really meant a *children's* party. The "grown-folk" left home on that day, and the children had free range of the house for their plays and rejoicing. So, through the ample rooms and the broad halls of the Van Rensselaer mansion the children's voices ring merrily, until, tired of romp and frolic, the little folks gather on the great staircase for rest and gossip. And here the fresh-faced little host, in a sky-blue silk coat lined with yellow, a white satin vest broidered with gold lace, white silk knee-breeches, and stockings tied with pink ribbons, pumps, ruffles, and frills, is listening intently while Mistress Margery, radiant in her tight-sleeved satin dress, peaked-toed and bespangled shoes, and wonderfully arranged hair, is telling the group of girls and boys all about General Burgoyne and the British officers, and how much they liked the real Dutch supper her mother gave them one day — "suppawn and malck [40] and rulliches, [41] with chocolate and soft waffles, you know," — and how General the Baron Riedesel had said that if they stayed till Christmas he would play at Saint Claes (Santa Claus) for them.

"Oh, Margery!" exclaimed Stephen, "you wouldn't have a Hessian for good old Saint Claes, would you?"

"Why not?" said Mistress Margery, with a toss of her pretty head. "Do you think you are the only patroon, my lord Stephen?"

For Santa Claus was known among the boys and girls of those old Dutch days as "the children's patroon" (*De Patroon van Kinder-vreugd*).

"I saw the Hessian baron t' other night, Margarita," said Stephen's best boy-friend, Abram Van Vechten; "he never could play at Santa Claus. He's not the right shape at all. And then a Hessian! Why, I'd sooner have old Balthazar!"

"Oh, dear, what a Saint Claes he'd make!" cried all the girls and boys, for old Balthazar Lydius was the terror of the Albany children in those days — "a tall, spare Dutchman, with a bullet head," a sort of Bluebeard to their imaginations, living in his "big mahogany house with carved beams," near the old *Kerk*, and scowling and growling at every *Kind* who passed his door.

"No, no, Abram," protested Margery, "I'd rather have the baron, even if he is a Hessian. Only imagine old Balthazar playing at Saint Claes, girls! Why, he's as sour as a ladle of Aunt Schuyler's *kool-slaa*. Show us how he looks, Stephen; you can, you know."

"Yes, do, do!" shouted all the girls and boys. "Show us Abram's sour face. Let's see which is the best patroon."

"Suppawn And Malck And Rulliches, With Chocolate And Soft Waffles, You Know," Said Mistress Margery.

So the boy lengthened down his face and pulled in his cheeks and looked so ferociously sour that the children fairly shrieked with delight at the caricature, and Abram cried: "That's it; that's old Balthazar as sure as you live! That's just the way he looked at me last winter when I almost ran into him as I was sliding down the long coast at Fort hill. My! I was so scared that I ran as fast as my legs could carry me from way below the *Kerk* clear past the Van der Hayden palace." [42]

But, in the midst of the laughter, a quick step sounded in the hall, and General Ten Broek came to the children-crowded staircase. "The Helderberg farmers are here, lad," he said to his nephew; and the young patroon, bidding his guests keep up the fun while he left them awhile, followed his uncle through the door-way and across the broad court-yard to where, just south of the manor-house, stood the rent-office. As the boy emerged from the mansion, the throng of tenants who had gathered there at his invitation gazed admiringly at the manly-looking little lad, resplendent in blue and yellow, and gold lace, and greeted him with a rousing birthday cheer — a loyal welcome to their boy patroon, their young *Opperhoofdt*, or chief.

"My friends," the lad said, acknowledging their greeting with a courtly bow, "I have asked you to come to the manor-house on this, my birthday, so that I might thank you for what you did for me before the Saratoga fight, when you sent so much of your stock and produce to the army simply on my order. But I wish also to give you something besides thanks. And so, that you may know how much I value your friendship and fealty, I have, with my guardian's approval, called you here to present to each one of you a free and clear title to all the lands you have, until now, held in fee from me as the patroon of Rensselaerswyck. General Ten Broek will give you the papers before you leave the office, and Pedrom has a goodly spread waiting for you in the lower hall. Take this from me, my friends, with many thanks for what you have already done for me."

Then, what a cheer went up! The loyal tenantry of the Helderberg farms had neither looked for nor expected any special return for their generous offerings to the army of the Congress, and this action of the boy patroon filled every farmer's heart with something more than gratitude; for now each one of them was a land-owner, as free and untrammelled as the boy patroon himself. And, as fair Portia says in the play,

"So shines a good deed in a naughty world,"

that, when young Stephen Van Rensselaer went joyfully back to his children's party, and the Helderberg farmers to black Pedrom's "spread" in the lower hall, it would have been hard to say which felt the happier — the giver or the receivers of this generous and manly gift.

The years of battle continued, but Dominie Doll's boarding-school, smoked out of 'Sopus when the British troops laid Kingston in ashes, found shelter in Hurley; and here the boys repaired for instruction — for school must go on though war rages and fire burns. The signs of pillage and desolation were all around them; but, boy-like, they thought little of the danger, and laughed heartily at Dominie Doll's story of the poor 'Sopus Dutchman who, terribly frightened at the sight of the red-coats, fled wildly across a deserted hay-field, and stepped suddenly upon the end of a long hay-rake left behind by the "skedaddling" farmers. Up flew the long handle of the rake and struck the terrified Dutchman a sounding whack upon the back of his head. He gave himself up for lost. "*Oh, mein Got, mein Got!*" he cried, dropping upon his knees and lifting imploring hands to his supposed captors, "I kivs up, I kivs up, mynheer soldiermans. Hooray for King Shorge!"

Nearly two years were passed here upon the pleasant hill-slopes that stretch away to the Catskill ridges and the rugged wildness of the Stony Clove; and then, in the fall of 1779, when the boy patroon had reached his fifteenth birthday, it was determined to send him, for still higher education, to the College of New Jersey, at Princeton. Of that eventful journey of the lad and his half-dozen school-fellows, under military escort, from the hills of the Upper Hudson to the shot-scarred college on the New Jersey plains, a most interesting story could be told. I doubt whether many, if any, boys ever went to school under quite such delightfully exciting circumstances. For their route lay through a war-worried section; past the dismantled batteries of Stony Point, where "Mad Anthony Wayne" had gained so much glory and renown; past the Highland fortresses, and through the ranks of the Continental Army, visiting General Washington at his headquarters at West Point, and carrying away never-forgotten recollections of the great commander; cautiously past roving bands of cruel "cow-boys" and the enemy's outposts around captured New York, to the battered college buildings which had alternately been barracks and hospital for American and British troops. And an equally interesting story could be told of the exciting college days when, almost within range of the enemy's guns, the boom of the distinct cannon would come like a punctuation in recitations, and the fear of fusillades would help a boy through many a "tight squeeze" in neglected lessons. But this was education under difficulties. The risk became too great, and the young patroon was finally transferred to the quieter walls of Harvard College, from which celebrated institution he graduated with honor in 1782, soon after his eighteenth birthday.

"The Throng Of Tenants Greeted Him With A Rousing Birthday Cheer."

The quiet life of an average American boy would not seem to furnish very much worth the telling. The boy patroon differed little, save in the way of birth and vast estate, from other boys and girls of the eventful age in which he lived; but many instances in his youthful career could safely be recorded. We might tell how he came home from college just as the great war was closing; how he made long trips, on horseback and afoot, over his great estate, acquainting himself with his tenantry and their needs; how, even before he was twenty years old, he followed the custom of his house and married fair Mistress Margery, the "brave girl" of the Schuyler mansion; and how, finally, on the first of November, 1785, all the tenantry of Rensselaerswyck thronged the grounds of the great manor-house, and, with speech and shout and generous barbecue, celebrated his coming of age — the twenty-first birthday of the boy patroon, — now no longer boy or patroon, but a free American citizen in the new Republic of the United States.

His after-life is part of the history of his State and of his country. At an early age he entered public life, and filled many offices of trust and responsibility. An assemblyman, a State Senator, a lieutenant-governor, a member of Congress, a major-general, and the conqueror of Queenstown in Canada in the War of 1812, one of the original projectors of the great Erie Canal, and, noblest of all, the founder and patron of a great school for boys, — the Rensselaer Polytechnic Institute at Troy, — he was, through all, the simple-hearted citizen and the noble-minded man. But no act in all his long life-time of seventy-five years became him better than the spirit in which he accepted the great change that made the great lord patroon of half a million acres the plain, untitled citizen of a free republic.

"Though born to hereditary honors and aristocratic rank," says his biographer, "with the history of the past before him, in possession of an estate which connected him nearly with feudal times and a feudal ancestry, and which constituted him in his boyhood a baronial proprietor, he found himself, at twenty-one, through a forcible and bloody revolution, the mere fee-simple owner of acres, with just such political rights and privileges as belonged to his own freehold tenantry, and no other." And though the Revolution, in giving his country independence, had stripped him of power and personal advantages, he accepted the change without regret, and preferred his position as one in a whole nation of freemen, to that feudal rank which he had inherited from generations of ancestors, as the Boy Patroon, the last Lord of the Manor of Rensselaerswyck.

From the patrician emperor of old Rome to the patrician citizen of modern America these sketches of Historic Boys have extended. They represent but a few from that long list of remarkable boys, who, through the ages, have left their mark upon their times, — lads who, even had they died "in their teens," would still have been worthy of record as "historic boys." The lessons of their lives are manifold. They tell of pride and selfishness, of tyranny and wasted power, of self-reliance and courage, of ambition and self-conquest, of patience and manliness. History is but the record of opportunities for action availed of or neglected. And opportunities are never wanting. They exist to-day in the cities of the New World, even as they did ages ago with young David in the valley of Elah, with the boy Marcus in the forum of Rome, or with the valiant young Harry of Monmouth striving for victory on the bloody field of Shrewsbury.

Whenever or wherever a manly boy says his word for justice and for right, or does his simple duty in a simple, straightforward way, regardless of consequences or of the world's far too-ready sneer or frown, the stamp of the hero may be seen; and however humble his condition or contracted his sphere there is in him the mettle and the possibilities that may make him, even though he know it not, a worthy claimant for an honored place on the world's record of Historic Boys.

THE END.

FOOTNOTES:

[38] The Fuyck, or fish-net, — an old Dutch name for Albany.

[39] Commissioners and sheriffs.

[40] Mush and milk.

[41] A kind of chopped meat.

[42] One of the old Dutch "show houses" of Albany 100 years ago.